MY VOICE WILL GO WITH YOU

EDITED AND WITH COMMENTARY
BY *Sidney Rosen*, M.D.

FOREWORD BY LYNN HOFFMAN
Ackerman Institute of Family Therapy

W · W · NORTON & COMPANY

NEW YORK · LONDON

My Voice Will Go with You THE TEACHING TALES

OF MILTON H. ERICKSON, M.D.

Printed in the United States of America.

The text of this book is composed in photocomposition Avanta. The typeface used for display is Palatino. Composition and manufacturing are by the Haddon Craftsmen. Book design by Marjorie J. Flock.

First published as a Norton paperback 1991

Library of Congress Cataloging in Publication Data
Erickson, Milton H.
 My voice will go with you.
 Bibliography: p.
 1. Psychotherapy. I. Rosen, Sidney, 1926–
II. Title.
RC480.5.E74 1982   616.89'14   81–18743
                              AACR2

ISBN 0–393–30135–4

W. W. Norton & Company, Inc. 500 Fifth Avenue, New York, N. Y. 10110
W. W. Norton & Company Ltd, 10 Coptic Street, London WC1A 1PU

3 4 5 6 7 8 9 0

To Estelle, Jeff, and Joanna. With all my love.

Contents

Foreword by Lynn Hoffman   13

Editor's Note   17

1. *Changing the Unconscious Mind*   25
   INTRAPSYCHIC CHANGE   29
   INTERPRETATIONS OF ERICKSON'S THERAPEUTIC
       APPROACHES   32
   APPLICATIONS OF THE TEACHING TALES IN THERAPY   34
   VICIOUS PLEASURE   36

2. *Motivating Tales*   46
   LEARNING TO STAND UP   47
   THE BOY WILL BE DEAD BY MORNING   52
   DILATATION   53
   QUARRELING   55

3. *Trust the Unconscious*   57
   I'D LEARNED MUCH   57
   LIGHT SNOW   57
   NARWHAL   58
   HE WILL TALK   58
   SCRATCHING HOGS   59
   SEVEN ASTERISKS   61
   CURIOUS   64
   PROFESSOR RODRIGUEZ   66
   HUEY DUCK, DEWEY DUCK, AND LOUIE DUCK   68

WALKING DOWN THE STREET   69
AUTOMATIC WRITING   71
TRANCES IN BALI   74

4. *Indirect Suggestion*   75
THE HYPNOTIC SUBJECT IS LITERAL   75
ORANGES   77
WALKING AROUND THE RESISTANCE   79
CACTI   80
COMPETITION   81
WET DREAMS   83
PRETEND A TRANCE   84
DO YOU HEAR IT?   86
SKIN CONDITIONS   87
"AUTO"-HYPNOSIS   88
DELVING   89
KATHLEEN: TREATMENT OF A PHOBIA   91

5. *Overcoming Habitual Limitations*   99
STONES AND QUANTUM MECHANICS   100
GOING FROM ROOM TO ROOM   101
I WIN OLYMPIC CHAMPIONSHIPS ALL THE TIME   102
DONALD LAWRENCE AND THE GOLD MEDAL   102
TRAINING THE U.S. RIFLE TEAM TO BEAT THE
    RUSSIANS   107
A FLASH OF COLOR   108
WALKING ON GLARE ICE   110
THE TARAHUMARA INDIANS   112
DRY BEDS   113
BOLO TIE   117
SIN   119
REDUCE—GAIN—REDUCE   123
A GORGEOUS WAY TO DIET   125
SIGHT-SEEING   126
YOUR ALCOHOLIC HAS TO BE SINCERE   128
A FRIENDLY DIVORCE   129

START THE BALL ROLLING 133
CLAUSTROPHOBIA 134
THE STARS ARE THE LIMIT 136
BLOOD ON THE KEYS 137

6. *Reframing* 143
RAISING THEIR BIGNESS 144
STYLE 145
THE EASIEST GIRL TO SEDUCE 145
WALK A MILE 149
WHISTLEBERRIES 151
CINNAMON FACE 152
PSORIASIS 154
NOT A SINGLE ERECTION 157
SLURP, SLURP, SLURP 158

7. *Learning by Experience* 162
BEING SIX YEARS OLD 162
DREAMING 162
SWIMMING 163
TAKE A TASTE 166

8. *Taking Charge of Your Life* 167
ON DEATH AND DYING 167
I WANT A PAIR 170
DISAGREEMENTS 172
WORKING HER WAY THROUGH COLLEGE 172
PEARSON'S BRICK 174
CALLUSES 176

9. *Capturing the Innocent Eye* 178
THINKING LIKE CHILDREN 179
GHOST ROGER 180
WHY DO YOU CARRY THAT CANE? 180
MAGIC SHOWS 181

10. *Observe: Notice Distinctions*   182
THE RIGHT PSYCHIATRIST   182
HOW WOULD YOU TEST A TWO-YEAR-OLD?   184
PABLUM   185
HOW MANY DIFFERENT WAYS?   186
A DIFFERENT SHADE OF GREEN   186
ABROAD   188
SNEEZING   190
MAGIC, THE SUPERNATURAL, AND ESP   191
FORTUNE-TELLERS   192
MIND READING   193
MAGIC TRICKS   194
ESP WITH J. B. RHINE   195
A CARD TRICK   196

11. *Treating Psychotic Patients*   198
INSIDE OUT   198
THE PATIENT WHO STOOD   199
TWO JESUS CHRISTS   201
HERBERT   202

12. *Manipulation and Future Orientation*   211
MANIPULATION   213
BERT AND COCOA   214
AUTHORIZATION   216
DOLORES   218
GETTING JEFF TO CALL   219
WHAT WOULD YOU DO IF I SLAMMED YOU?   221
DACHSHUND AND GERMAN SHEPHERD   222
DERAIL THEM   222
LANCE AND COOKIE   223
US CRIPPLES   226
BLANK PAPER   228
RUTH   229
SALAAM   231
GLOBUS HYSTERICUS   233
OATS   235
GROWTH   236

13. *Teaching Values and Self-Discipline* 238

I DON'T HAS TO 238
GARBAGE 240
HEIDI-HO, THE SIX-YEAR-OLD KLEPTOMANIAC 241
EASTER BUNNY LETTERS 243
ROBERT—HE DOES IT WELL 244
SATURDAY CLASSES ON SUNDAY 248
JILL, HER OWN STYLE 250
SPANKING 251
SLAMMING DOORS 252

Bibliography 254

Foreword

Milton Erickson's teaching tales—the stories he told his patients and the stories he told the pilgrims who came to sit at his feet —are ingenious and enchanting. They are extraordinary examples of the art of persuasion. Some people would say that they are much too good to be tucked away on the psychiatry shelf, since even though their intention was therapeutic, they are part of a much larger tradition: the American tradition of wit and humor whose greatest exemplar is Mark Twain.

I first became aware of the amazing exploits of Erickson when I began to work as a writer and editor at the Mental Research Institute in Palo Alto in 1963. I was putting together the material for the book *Techniques of Family Therapy* with Jay Haley. Haley, who had taped hours of conversation with Erickson, told me story after story about him, while I listened entranced. This was part of my initiation into the field of family therapy, and it made a big impact on me. It is all the more an honor, then, eighteen years later, to be asked to write the foreword to Sidney Rosen's compilation of Erickson's teaching tales.

Because of the curious way Erickson stands on the line between healer and poet, scientist and bard, it is difficult to describe his work. Transcripts of his seminars, though wonderful, are to some extent unsatisfying. The written word simply cannot convey the pauses, smiles, and piercing upward glances with which Erickson punctuates his narratives, nor can it record his mastery of voice and tone. The written word, in short, cannot give any idea of the way Erickson *insinuates* himself.

Sidney Rosen has solved this problem, although I am not sure how he has done it. Erickson chose him, as disciple, as colleague, and as friend, to edit this volume. His intuition, as usual, was correct. Rosen has a way of taking you by the hand and *insinuating* you into Erickson's presence. There seems to be no obstruction. I once watched an underwater swimming show in Florida. The audience sat in an underground amphitheater that was separated by a pane of glass from a limestone spring. The water was so clear and transparent that the fish that swam close to the glass seemed to be gliding through air.

Reading this book was a similar experience, perhaps because Rosen gives us such a strong sense of the relational field that was Erickson's own natural medium. The first line of the first chapter is a remark from Erickson to Rosen on the nature of the unconscious. Just as Erickson weaves into his tales reminiscences, personal biography, odd thoughts, or unusual facts, so Rosen weaves into his commentary bits about this or that personal encounter with Erickson, associations to some particular tale, and ways he himself has used these stories in his own work with patients, and he also gives a running explication of the various techniques exemplified by the tales. The commentary *is* the relational field in which the stories are suspended.

In addition, Rosen seems to be speaking, not writing, again paralleling Erickson, and his style is friendly and nontechnical. It is also quite plain. Whether deliberately or not, Rosen creates a frame that is neutral enough to highlight the color and brilliance of the stories. Nevertheless, the totality transcends the effect of any one element. Thoughtful attention is paid to each anecdote, and a skilled and experienced hypnotherapist who himself is a gifted practitioner of Ericksonian techniques gives us a book that is, in effect, a teaching tale about a teaching tale.

Let me give a sense here of the way the commentary flows in and out of the tales, taking the first part of Chapter Three, "Trust the Unconscious," as my source. This chapter begins with a short anecdote about Erickson's having to give a speech on the spur of the moment and saying to himself that he didn't have to prepare, because he had confidence in the storehouse of ideas and experience he had built up over the years. Rosen underlines this theme of trust in one's unconsciously stored powers, and then includes a short vignette, "Light Snow," haunting in its simplicity, about a childhood memory and the memory of when that memory was laid down. This story is followed by two more on the same theme. The last story is about Erickson's not talking when he was four, and his mother's saying to people made uncomfortable by this fact, "When the time arrives, then he will talk." Rosen cuts back in briefly to say that this story is a good one to use with patients just learning how to go into trance.

The next story is splendid. It is called "Scratching Hogs." It describes a time when Erickson, who as a young man sold books to pay his way through college, was trying to sell some to a crusty old farmer. The man isn't having any and tells Erickson to go about his business. Erickson, without thinking, picks up some shingles from the ground and starts scratching the backs of the hogs the farmer is feeding. The farmer changes his mind and agrees to buy Erickson's books because, as he says, "You know how to scratch hogs."

This is followed by Rosen's commenting on the story and moving on to the occasion when he first heard it—after he had asked Erickson why he chose Rosen to write the foreword to his book *Hypnotherapy*. After explaining just what things about Rosen had made him wish to entrust the writing of a foreword to him, Erickson added, "I like the way you scratch a hog."

This fragment gives an idea of the tapestried richness of the book. Each tale is treated as a precious object in a collection, full of memories, and Rosen shares with the reader the different meanings they evoke for him, both as a person and as a clinician. If I were a canny fellow like that farmer, I would buy this book. Sidney Rosen does know how to scratch a hog.

LYNN HOFFMAN

Ackerman Institute of Family Therapy

Editor's Note

On Thursday, March 27, 1980, my New York office called me and gave me the news that Milton Erickson had died. I was on a skiing vacation in Snowbird, Utah. My first thoughts were of Betty Erickson, and I called her. I learned that Erickson had finished his regular week of teaching on Friday, had autographed twelve books, and on Saturday had been somewhat tired during the day. Early Sunday morning, he suddenly stopped breathing. Betty Erickson applied artificial respiration and reinstated his breathing. A paramedic squad worked with her and took him to the hospital, where his blood pressure, which showed a systolic level of about forty, could not be elevated, even with the help of dopamine infusions. It was determined that Erickson was suffering from "septic shock." A beta-streptococcus infection was diagnosed, and it was manifested as a peritonitis. He did not respond to massive doses of antibiotics.

Erickson's family congregated from all over the United States. It is a very devoted and large one, consisting of four sons and four daughters, along with grandchildren and great-grandchildren. Family members stayed with him while he was in a semicomatose state. From their accounts, it appears probable that he died as he had often said he wanted to—with a smile on his face, surrounded by friends and family. He was seventy-eight years old.

About the funeral services, Betty Erickson said, "Don't put yourself out, Sid. It will only be a small gathering. And I know that some people are planning memorial services in different cities." Fortunately, I was able to drive to the Salt Lake City airport and arrive in Phoenix after a short flight. The calm and warmth of the Phoenix day was in marked contrast to the windy cold of the mountain I had just left.

It *was* only a small gathering. Erickson's body had been cremated, and the ashes were to be scattered on Squaw Peak. Four people spoke at the service—Jeffrey Zeig, Robert Pearson, Kay Thompson, and Ernest Rossi. I recall Pearson's final comment: "Erickson took on the psychiatric establishment single-handedly, and he beat them. They don't know it yet . . ." Rossi recited the dream in song and verse, that had awakened him in tears just before he had received the phone call from Phoenix, with the news of Erickson's death.

After the services, Betty Erickson said that she had something for me. It was an exchange of letters between Erickson and Salvador Minuchin. Minuchin had met Erickson for the first time only about a week before his death. Erickson had never read the last letter, but Betty Erickson had dutifully answered it. She had asked Minuchin for permission for me to use his letters in this book, and Minuchin had graciously agreed.

The last letter begins, "My meeting with you was one of those memorable experiences. In my lifetime, I have met a handful of extraordinary people—you are one of them."

It continues, "I was tremendously impressed with the way in which you are able to look at simple moments and describe their complexity, and at your trust in the capacity of human beings to harness a repertory of experiences they do not know they have."

During my visit to Phoenix in 1979, I had been invited to sleep in the small cottage that is adjacent to Erickson's office. I took the opportunity to look through books in his library and was impressed that many of these books had been inscribed to him by their authors, with messages of gratitude. These books dealt with many fields—not only with the fields of hypnosis and psycho-therapy. For example, there were books about Gurdjieff, about city planning, and about literature. The authors' inscriptions to Erickson often bordered on the ecstatic—such as "Thank you for teaching me the difference between knowledge and knowing."

To those, like myself, who have been following the works of Erickson since the 1940s and 1950s, it was gratifying to know that as he was nearing the age of eighty, he was finally recognized by a larger audience and that his techniques and approaches would be of benefit to many more people. Of course, in professional hypnosis circles, Erickson had long been known as a leader. He was the founding editor of the American Society of Clinical Hypnosis. In the 1950s he wrote the article on hypnosis for the *Encyclopaedia Britannica.* Professionals often called upon him for advice on hypnosis and altered states of consciousness. He hyp-notized Aldous Huxley in the 1950s and collaborated with him on his study of altered states of consciousness. Margaret Mead studied with him for more than forty years and, in fact, became a member of the Society of Clinical Hypnosis. In the 1940s *Life* magazine discussed Erickson's work. In 1952 he was an active participant in the Macy Conferences, during which authorities like Gregory Bateson, Margaret Mead, and Lawrence Kubie, the eminent psychoanalyst, discussed matters that led to the forma-tion of the field of cybernetics. Still, most lay people and even many psychotherapists had never heard of him; when the name "Erickson" was mentioned, they would usually say, "Oh, yes, Erik Erikson?"

An upsurge of interest in Milton Erickson was stimulated by the writings of Jay Haley, who studied with Erickson for seven-teen years and became a leader in the field of family therapy. More recently, Erickson's ideas have been spread by the writings and workshops of Richard Bandler and John Grinder.

A long list of candidates wished to attend the group meetings held by Erickson. Anyone calling Erickson in his last year was told that there was a wait of over one year and that no further reservations would be made until after the International Congress on Ericksonian Hypnosis, which was to be held in Phoenix in December 1980.

When I presented his work to professional audiences, with demonstrations of hypnosis, sometimes with the aid of videotapes, I found that many were eager to visit Erickson themselves. Since this was impossible for most, I wondered what aspect of his teaching would best give them, and others, a sense of personal contact with him, while conveying the essence of his therapeutic approaches.

I recalled a conversation in 1978, between Erickson and one of the psychiatrists who attended his seminars. At one point Erickson had turned to the psychiatrist and, with a slight smile, had asked, "Do you still think that therapy is just telling stories?" Now, it is obvious that even though Erickson's therapy was not *only* "telling stories," the telling of what I call his "teaching tales" was one of the major elements in his therapy.

In August of 1979, Milton Erickson gave me permission to write a book on his "teaching tales." By November he had agreed to be co-author of the book, and our publishing contract was signed about three months before his death.

The "teaching tales" are stories that Erickson told to patients and students over the years. For the last six years or so of his life he met with groups of psychotherapists almost every day, for uninterrupted four- or five-hour sessions, during which he would discuss hypnosis, therapy, and life and would generously call on "teaching tales."

Most of the names in the stories that follow have been changed, except for those of members of the Erickson family, since I was assured that the latter had no objection to the use of their names. Throughout the book, unless gender is specified, I have referred to the patient or student as "he," since constant use of "he or she" would be unwieldy. This is a case where our pronouns have not yet caught up with our raised consciousness.

Thanks are due to Elaine Rosenfeld, Dava Weinstein, and Joan Poelvoorde for help in obtaining material; to Ernest Rossi for support and encouragement; and to Jeffrey Zeig for generous donation of both his time and invaluable ideas. Betty Erickson deserves special thanks—for her trust that I would not vulgarize Milton's work, for the days she spent going over the manuscript and family tales, and for insisting on accuracy, even in the smallest details. Any lapses from her standards are, of course, my responsibility.

SIDNEY ROSEN, M.D.

New York, 1981

And I want you to choose some time in the past when you were a very, very little girl. And my voice will go with you. And my voice will change into that of your parents, your neighbors, your friends, your schoolmates, your playmates, your teachers. And I want you to find yourself sitting in the school room, a little girl feeling happy about something, something that happened a long time ago, that you forgot a long time ago.

— Milton H. Erickson

A man wanted to know about mind, not in nature, but in his private, large computer. He asked it (no doubt in his best Fortran), "Do you compute that you will ever think like a human being?" The machine then set to work to analyze its own computational habits. Finally, the machine printed its answer on a piece of paper, as such machines do. The man ran to get the answer and found, neatly typed, the words: THAT REMINDS ME OF A STORY.

— Gregory Bateson, *Mind and Nature*

1. *Changing the Unconscious Mind*

"What you don't realize, Sid, is that most of your life is unconsciously determined." When Erickson said this to me, I reacted as many of my patients do when I say the same thing. I felt that he meant my life was predetermined, and that the most I could hope for was to become aware of the unconscious patternings that were firmly set. However, I realized later that the unconscious is not necessarily unchangeable. All of the experiences that we have today affect our unconscious mind as well as our conscious mind. If I read something that inspires me, my unconscious mind has been changed. If I have a meeting with an important person— that is, a person who is important to me—my unconscious is changed. In fact, the positive value of any psychotherapy is obviously based on the ability of a person to change, largely as the result of an encounter with another person or persons.

In my opinion, this change is accomplished most effectively and permanently when the therapist focuses on influencing his patient's unconscious patterns, which frequently include his values and frames of reference. Erickson agreed with this point of view. Toward the end of his life he developed a very effective approach to accomplish this goal—his teaching seminars.

The last time I saw him, he explained to me how this approach had developed.

"I had to spend too much time on one patient. I would rather teach a *lot* of people how to think, how to handle problems. I have dozens and dozens of letters saying, 'You have completely changed my way of treating patients.' I get a lot of patients, but I see them less. I see more patients and I see them for shorter times."

I questioned, "And this is the result of . . . ?"

He answered, "Their coming here and letting me tell them stories. Then they go home and alter their practice."

Obviously "coming here and letting me tell them stories" involved expectations and communications on many levels. For example, anyone who spent time with Erickson was likely to experience various levels of hypnotic trance. With positive expectations, in a trance, we are most open to the messages and influences transmitted in Erickson's stories. Erickson believed that if the listener "forgot" a story—developed an amnesia for it—its effect could be even more potent.

In "telling stories" Erickson was, of course, following an ancient tradition. Since time immemorial, stories have been used as a way of transmitting cultural values, ethics, and morality. A bitter pill can be swallowed more easily when it is embedded in a sweet matrix. A straight moral preachment might be dismissed, but guidance and direction become acceptable when embedded in a story that is intriguing, amusing, and interestingly told. Toward this end, Erickson's tales utilize many effective storytelling devices, including the use of humor and the inclusion of interesting information, such as little-known medical, psychological, and anthropological facts. Therapeutic suggestions are interspersed in stories whose content is far removed both from the patient's concerns and the therapist's overt focus.

Trance, according to Erickson, is the state in which learning and openness to change are most likely to occur. It does not refer to an induced somnolent state. Patients are not "put under" by the therapist, nor are they out of control and directed by the will of another person. Trance, in fact, is a natural state experienced by everyone. Our most familiar experience takes place when we daydream, but other trance states can occur when we meditate, pray, or perform exercises—such as jogging, which has sometimes been called "meditation in motion." In these situations, a person is aware of the vividness of inner mental and sensory experiences, and external stimuli, such as sounds and movements, assume lesser importance.

In trance, patients often intuitively understand the meaning of dreams, symbols, and other unconscious expressions. They are closer to what Erickson called "unconscious learnings," less involved with thoughts and issues. They may accept the hypnotist's suggestions with reduced critical sense, yet if these suggestions conflict with patients' values, acceptance will not occur or is transient. Amnesia may be present for part or all of the trance experience but is by no means an essential aspect of trance.

In helping a patient enter a trance, the therapist captures the patient's attention and directs it inward, leading him to an inner search and a hypnotic response. The hypnotic response, which is related both to the patient's needs and expectations and to the therapist's direction, is derived from the patient's "vast storehouse of learning." In order to achieve this response, therapeutic suggestions may be indirect, interspersed in an ordinary conversation or an interesting tale. More specific helpful approaches have been described in *Hypnotherapy*, by Erickson and Ernest Rossi.

The therapist is alert to subtle changes that indicate a patient's "response attentiveness." These include a flattening of facial expression, staring, absence of blinking, and almost complete immobility. When this constellation is noted, the therapist can safely assume that his patient has entered a light trance. He may then present a suggestion or simply say something like "That's it. Stay with that," knowing that the patient is likely to be dealing with material from the unconscious.

The tales often follow archetypal patterns, as seen in fairy tales, Biblical tales, and folk myths. As in folk myths, many of them include the theme of a quest. The accomplishment of one of Erickson's assigned tasks may not have the heroic drama of the Golden Fleece, but the inner drama and feelings of accomplishment are comparable. And there is something peculiarly American about many of his stories, especially those about his family. For this reason, Erickson has been called an American folk hero.

Still, one might wonder how listening to a story, even in a hypnotic trance, can help a patient or a student. The effect, in many ways, is similar to the "glow" one may feel after seeing a good movie. During the movie, many of us enter into an altered state of consciousness. We identify with one or more of the characters, and we leave "trance-formed." However, this feeling lasts for only a short time—ten or fifteen minutes at most. By contrast, people find themselves, many years later, referring back to an Erickson tale. Their behavior and attitudes may be permanently changed.

Erickson explained these permanent changes by the fact that they occurred in the context of "hypnosis," which he defined as "the evocation and utilization of unconscious learnings." When a therapist is able, with or without the use of stories, to help a patient get in touch with his own unutilized knowledge, that patient is most likely to incorporate these forgotten learnings into his behavior. More constructive and self-reinforcing behavior may often result.

How is this process different from "brainwashing"? Perhaps the main difference is that without cultural reinforcement "brainwashing" tends to fade away. During the Korean War, for example, many "brainwashed" American prisoners-of-war were led to accept anti-American beliefs. In fact, thousands wanted to remain in Communist China rather than return home. Yet after they had been repatriated, it would seem, most, if not all, returned to their former beliefs.

Erickson's interventions were more likely to lead to changes that were self-reinforcing and led to further changes. Perhaps this occurred because these changes were in the direction of growth and "opening." Of course, they were likely to be most effective and permanent in a culture that supported Erickson's philosophy —that the individual is important, that he can better himself, and that each of us has unique possibilities for growth.

INTRAPSYCHIC CHANGE

As already mentioned, the unconscious mind can be influenced by positive input. Involvement with a therapist like Erickson, who is optimistic and supportive of growth, can in itself constitute positive input. The addition of "teaching tales" reinforces, supplements, and directs that positive input. In the telling of stories, Erickson adds new data, evokes new feelings, and prescribes new experiences. A patient who has been struggling for years within a guilt-ridden, narrow view of life may be presented through these tales with Erickson's permissive, life-celebrating philosophy. These views reach him on many levels, including the unconscious. They may be presented to the patient in the waking state and the hypnotic state. The patient may then discover that he does not have to rely solely on his own well-established circular patterns of thought. He does not have to "make do" with his own limited philosophy and limited mental sets. Partly through the medium of these stories, he becomes aware of new possibilities, which he is free to accept or reject on both conscious and unconscious levels.

Sometimes the patient will identify with a character in a story, or with Erickson himself—the master, who can deal successfully with difficult challenges. He may then experience a sense of accomplishment. This sense of accomplishment allows him to approach a situation with a greater feeling of confidence. This can

be illustrated in the treatment of sexual problems, such as premature ejaculation. When a patient has been able to experience
himself successfully enjoying a sexual act while in a hypnotic
trance, the therapist has added to his memories the feeling of
success and the expectation of further success.

Of course, not all of Erickson's teaching tales, and certainly
not all parts of all tales, are aimed at adding such positive input
to the unconscious. Some of them are meant to stir up and bring
to awareness feelings of deadness, feelings of being stuck, or
feelings of lack of authenticity. The listener then must tap his
own unconscious resources in order to ameliorate the situation.
Or he may find emotional and intellectual sustenance in one of
the other Erickson tales.

A single remembered phrase from one of Erickson's stories
may change the feeling of an entire day. On one occasion, this
happened to me while I was walking beside a meadow. Suddenly
the sentence "Did you know that every blade of grass is a different
shade of green?" popped into my head and I looked at the grass
more closely. Indeed, it was true! For the rest of the day, I walked
around with my eyes more open than usual.

Many of Erickson's tales appear to involve interactions and
even manipulations between people. One might conclude that he
is teaching people how to manipulate others. This is far from the
intent of the stories, or their effect, which is manifested mostly
in inner changes. Many people who have heard these stories find
themselves functioning with increased freedom and creativity.
This obviously comes from some intrapsychic changes. We can
better understand these changes if we look at the stories and their
characters as representing inner psychic structures. For example,
parents in the stories can represent guides, sources of love and
support, or sources of irrational guidance. More often they represent sources of irrational coercive force. A child in a story can
represent the child within us—inexperienced, eager to learn but

not knowing how, spontaneous but ignorant, with a limited repertoire of behaviors and responses. When the reader identifies with
the child, he is likely to feel hopeful as he hears how the child
overcomes blockages to growth and freedom.

Some intrapsychic changes may result from the process of
"reparenting." Erickson used this concept in a broader way than
had Jacqui Lee Schiff in her book *Transactional Analysis Treatment of Psychosis*. Erickson applied the term to his method of
replacing previous "parental" injunctions with new ideas, which
he instilled by means of posthypnotic suggestions.

These posthypnotic suggestions might be facilitated by a
phrase that Erickson often included in his hypnotic inductions:
"And my voice will go with you wherever you are." This phrase
enabled him to keep contact with the patient in trance, regardless
of the depth of the patient's regression, while also serving as a cue
to posthypnotic suggestions. Another cueing phrase might be
"You will see a flash of color." Subsequently, long after the therapeutic session, whenever the patient saw a flash of color, he was
likely to respond to other posthypnotic suggestions given in conjunction with the "flash of color" suggestion. These suggestions
could include injunctions and points of view, which would then
be "heard" (often in Erickson's voice) as the voice of an in-
trojected parent or superego. This introjection of the therapist's
voice can occur in any psychotherapy but is most likely to occur
when the patient is in a hypnotic trance. One possible explanation
for this phenomenon was given by Lawrence Kubie at a meeting
of the American Psychoanalytic Association. Dr. Kubie noted
that in a hypnotic trance the distinction between hypnotist and
subject is abolished. The subject then hears the hypnotist's voice
as if it were coming from inside his own head—as his own inner
voice. This was true of Erickson. His voice would become your
voice, and his voice would go with you, wherever you were.

Obviously, the best way of conveying the full impact of these tales would be to present them through videotape, or, at least, audiotape. One would certainly have a better sense of the importance of Erickson's changes of voice, pauses, body position, and nonverbal cues. Unfortunately, rather few videotapes are available at this time. The intelligibility of most audiotapes is poor. In fact, one advantage of having the stories printed out is that they are more easily available for study and review.

INTERPRETATIONS OF ERICKSON'S THERAPEUTIC APPROACHES

Erickson's case reports often appear to present magical cures, and some people have reacted by not believing them. Others feel that they are fictional reports—interestingly written and presented, but fiction nevertheless. From personal observation of Erickson while he was working with patients, I can attest that at least some of the reports are not fiction. In fact, I believe that all of them are quite factual and were edited only for the sake of a more readable, and perhaps more dramatic, presentation than is found in most clinical reports. Some who *believe* that Erickson effected dramatic and real changes in patients, students, and therapists still maintain that these results were probably obtained because of some special Ericksonian charisma that could not be transmitted to other therapists. Recently, however, there have been attempts to study his modes of communication in a more analytical way.

In *Uncommon Therapy*, Jay Haley emphasizes the strategic aspect. Haley has defined "strategic therapy" as one in which "the clinician initiates what happens during therapy and designs a particular approach for each problem." Haley points out that Erickson communicates with patients, not only in metaphors, but that he also "works within the metaphor to bring about a change." He notes that Erickson avoids interpretations and that he would feel that "typical 'insight' interpretations of unconscious communications are absurdly reductionistic, like summarizing a Shakespearean play in a sentence." Haley has also pointed out that major features of Ericksonian therapy include "encouraging resistance," "providing a worse alternative," "encouraging a response by frustrating it," "seeding ideas," "amplifying a deviation," and "prescribing the symptom."

Bandler and Grinder, with their "neurolinguistic" approach, have interpreted Erickson's communication in a microscopic way. They have noted, for example, his tendency to "mark" suggestions, which he may intersperse within a story. This "marking" is done, for example, by pausing, by changing his position or tone of voice. It may also be accomplished by preceding the "marked" suggestion with the insertion of the patient's name.

Ernest Rossi, in *Hypnotic Realities* and *Hypnotherapy*, has broken down Erickson's hypnotic inductions and indirect forms of suggestion into five stages: (1) fixation of attention, (2) depotentiating habitual frameworks and belief systems, (3) unconscious search, (4) unconscious process, and (5) hypnotic response. Each stage leads to the next. Rossi and his co-author, Erickson himself, have designated their approach as the "Utilization Approach to Hypnotherapy." In these books and in Watzlawick's works *The Language of Change* and *Change*, there is discussion of the thesis that Erickson communicates with the right brain, with its tendency to deal primarily in terms of primary processes, archaic language, emotions, space, and form (i.e., images).

Jeffrey Zeig, in *A Teaching Seminar with Milton H. Erickson*, lists some of the values of using anecdotes in therapy as follows: (1) anecdotes are nonthreatening; (2) anecdotes are engaging; (3) anecdotes foster independence: the individual needs to make sense out of the message and then come to a self-initiated conclusion or a self-initiated action; (4) anecdotes can be used to bypass natural resistance to change; (5) anecdotes can be used to control the relationship; (6) anecdotes model flexibility; (7) anecdotes can create confusion and promote hypnotic responsiveness; and (8) anecdotes tag the memory—"they make the presented idea more memorable."

APPLICATIONS OF THE TEACHING TALES IN THERAPY

One of Erickson's most important and useful approaches could be called "mind reading." By observing the patient carefully and by mirroring his behavior and responses, Erickson gives the patient the feeling that his mind is being read and that Erickson really knows him. This kind of "knowing" leads to a very intimate relationship. "Rapport," which is imperative in all kinds of psychotherapy, is apparently formed more quickly during hypnotic therapy than in other forms of psychotherapy. (In this regard, it is of interest that Anton Mesmer was the first one to use the term "rapport" in conjunction with therapy.) Most therapists, regardless of their "school," will agree that this rapport, the "doctor-patient relationship," is of central importance. A strong therapeutic relationship leads the patient to feel understood, safe, and secure. With this support he may then venture into both inner and outer worlds with greater confidence and with a greater readiness to take risks.

The type of "knowing" referred to here is quite different from the usual way in which an analytic therapist gets to know "about" a patient. In fact, it was not necessary for Erickson to acquire a great deal of information about a patient's background, or even about his symptoms. There is some truth to the speculation that his knowing was "intuitive," but only if we understand that Erickson's intuition was grounded in years of careful and painstaking training in observing. His observations pertained not only to simple matters such as body movements, breathing, and pulse rate (seen in the neck), but also to the patient's responses, as he listened to the tales. For example, if a patient tightened up at a certain point in a story, this was a clue that some relevant point had been touched upon. Erickson might then utilize another story, or elaborate on the same one, in ways that enhanced the patient's responsiveness. Thus, the stories are not only therapeutic but also diagnostic.

The teaching tales were always used and must always be applied in conjunction with other principles of Ericksonian therapy. These principles include those that have been outlined by Haley and others, such as symptom prescription, utilization of the resistance, and reframing. Activities, and even ordeals, are often prescribed. Change occurs as a result of the interaction between these activities and inner psychic shifting, in the context of a close and trusting doctor-patient relationship.

As he states in the book *Hypnotherapy*, Erickson applied the principles of getting the patient's attention through surprise, shock, doubt, and confusion, with the generous use of implications, questions, puns, and humor in his stories. Each story has a structure and plot, often with a surprise ending. The stories often build to a climax, followed by a feeling of relief or success. The use of the teaching tales demonstrates a principle that Erickson outlined in *Hypnotic Realities*, that is: "When dealing with a problem of difficulty make an interesting design out of it. Then you can concentrate on the interesting design and ignore the back-breaking labor involved." First, you identify an interesting design in the patient's responses and symptoms. Next you select a tale or tales that provide first an analogue of the patient's designs and then a better design. Or, as Erickson told his daughter-in-law, "Cookie," "First you model the patient's world. Then you role-model the patient's world." The following tale, "Vicious Pleasure," gives an example.

VICIOUS PLEASURE

A woman in her thirties arrived and said, "I don't suppose you want to see me." I said, "That's your supposition, would you like to hear mine?"

"Well," she said, "I am not deserving of your attention. When I was six years old my father molested me sexually and from the age of six until seventeen he used me as a sexual object, regularly, several times a week. And every time he did it I was in a state of fear. I was frozen with terror. I felt dirty, inferior, inadequate, ashamed.

"I thought, at seventeen, I had enough strength to break away from him and I worked my way through the rest of high school, hoping that that would give me a feeling of self-respect, and it didn't. Then I thought maybe a bachelor-of-arts degree would give me a feeling of self-respect. I worked my way through college. I felt ashamed, inferior, indecent. It was a terrible feeling of disappointment. I thought maybe a master's degree would give me self-respect, but it didn't. And all through college and graduate school I was propositioned. And that proved I didn't deserve self-respect. And I thought I would enroll for a doctorate degree, and men kept propositioning me. I just gave up and became a common prostitute. But that's not very nice. And some man offered to let me live with him. Well, a girl needs to have food and shelter so I agreed to it.

"Sex was a horrible experience. A penis is so hard and looks so threatening. I just became fear stricken and passive. And it was a painful, horrible experience. This man got tired of me and I began living with another man. The same thing over and over, and now I come to you. I feel like filth. An erect penis just terrifies me and I just get helpless, and weak, and passive. I am so glad when a man finishes.

"But I still have to live. I have to have clothes. I have to have shelter; and essentially I am not worth anything else."

I said, "That's an unhappy story; and the really unhappy part is—you're stupid! You tell me that you are afraid of a bold, erect, hard penis—and that's stupid! *You* know you have a vagina; *I* know it. A vagina can take the biggest, boldest, most assertive penis and turn it into a dangling, helpless object.

"And your vagina can *take a vicious pleasure in reducing it to a helpless dangling object.*"

The change on her face was wonderful. She said, "I am going to go back to Los Angeles, and can I see you in a month's time?" And I said, "Certainly." She came back in a month's time and said, "You're right! I went to bed with a man and I took a vicious pleasure in reducing him to helplessness. It didn't take long, and I enjoyed it. And I tried another man. The same thing. And another man. And it's pleasurable! Now I am going to get my Ph.D. and go into counseling, and I am going to wait until I see a man I want to live with."

I called her stupid. I *really* got her attention. And then I said, "Vicious pleasure." And she *did* resent men. I also said "pleasure."

When Erickson told me this tale I commented, "The way you described that hard penis, you made it sound very attractive; also —intriguing. Because there was also some verbal seduction. You were penetrating her verbally and imaginatively."

The first part of the tale, ending with "I am not worth anything else," is a modeling of the patient's world. If this tale is told to a patient who has tried unsuccessfully to overcome self-hate by means of external changes (getting college degrees, letting herself be used by others) and that patient is also threatened by some phobic stimulus (as represented by a "hard, threatening penis"), there is a good possibility, at least on an unconscious level, that there will be a recognition that the story parallels the patient's world.

The second phase, "role-modeling the patient's world," is accomplished after Erickson has acquired the patient's attention. Of course, if one were telling this story, attention would already have been won by the dramatic and shocking introduction. The attention is guaranteed with the use of words such as "vagina," "bold, erect, hard penis," and "stupid."

The actual role modeling is presented not only by the content of Erickson's suggestions, but also by his light and humorous attitude, as he restates and reframes the problem and then presents a reframed way of looking at the behavior that the patient was exhibiting, in her attempts to "live." The problem—fear of men and self-hate—is restated as "You tell me you're afraid of a bold, erect, hard penis." The word "afraid" condenses her fear, not only of men, but also of life. She is firmly told that this fear is "stupid" (and she is accustomed to thinking of herself as stupid). The sentence "And that bold, hard penis can enter your vagina" is a posthypnotic suggestion, which, when followed, will recall to the patient a somewhat maternal, whimsical view of the previously threatening penis—the "bold, hard penis," which he has mocked by repetition of the phrase.

The final, elegant step of reframing for the patient is expressed in the sentence "And your vagina can take a *vicious pleasure* in reducing it to a helpless dangling object."

For the reader, the final stage in role modeling is the resolution or cure, which, in this case, Erickson has the patient describe. When he, or when someone else, tells the tale, we are left with a hope that problems of this sort can be solved. As I have suggested, "problems of this sort" would not be limited to sexual difficulties resulting from incest, but might include phobic fears,

CHANGING THE UNCONSCIOUS MIND

anxiety-provoking situations, or problems with assertiveness. The metaphors in this tale provide many "pegs" on which problems of assertiveness, anger, and helplessness may be hung.

"Vicious Pleasure" is a beautiful example of the use of reframing to change a feeling of passive helplessness to one of active mastery. It also demonstrates how reframing can be used to help someone to move into the "one-up" position. Although the patient emphasized her fear and helplessness, Erickson recognized that she also had a strong feeling of resentment toward men. He tied this feeling of resentment to a potential feeling of pleasure and came up with the evocative phrase "vicious pleasure."

After reading this story, will we be more inclined to own up to feelings of resentment and take responsibility? Will we be better able to reach out toward the forces that we feel are pressuring us, and get pleasure from mastering them and reducing them to helplessness?

A therapist who uses Erickson's teaching tales is likely to experience a lessening of his own customary anxiety. Hence, he will be better able to focus on the business at hand—helping the patient to be more open, to find novel solutions and new frames of reference. Simply having a repertoire of stories can give the therapist a feeling of mastery, control, and competence. Also, as he reads or tells an Erickson tale, the therapist is likely to enter into a trance himself, either because of his associations to Erickson or because of the intrinsic "hypnotic effect" of the story. In the trance state the therapist will not only be less anxious; he will also be more open to his own unconscious associations. Therefore, he will be better able to help the patient lose *his* own anxieties, explore his inner potentials, and find different ways of viewing situations.

I have found that the best way for the therapist to select stories is through his own free associations. By this I mean not only cognitive free associations, but also bodily responses, emotions, perceptions, and, particularly, imagery associations. Here is an example of my use of Erickson's stories in the treatment of two different patients.

The first patient, a thirty-year-old Hasidic Jew, had been referred to me by his wife. She had read about Erickson's treatment techniques and felt I might be able to help her husband overcome his long-term inability to awaken at a reasonable hour. Since he was in the tenth grade at the Yeshiva, he had never been able to awaken before 11 A.M. or 12 noon. Because of this, he had been unable to hold a job but made a good adaptation in a family business. He had been married for about one year, and his wife now found it annoying and inconvenient to spend an hour trying to wake him up every morning.

During our first session, the patient told me that he had been hypnotized several times by a well-known hypnotherapist. The hypnotherapist was satisfied that the patient was hypnotized, but he himself was not. I put him through a standard hypnotic induction procedure, using arm-levitation and eye-fixation techniques. He was able to achieve both eye closure and a feeling of heaviness in his arm. However, at the end of the session he insisted that he was not hypnotized, that he had been merely cooperative, in spite of my caution that he try *not* to be cooperative. After this first session, he phoned me. He said that when his wife heard about our hypnotic procedure, she doubted it was really "uncommon" enough to qualify as an Ericksonian approach.

At our second session, I immediately told the patient, "We have already determined that you cannot be hypnotized to *your* satisfaction, even though both the other hypnotist and I thought that you were hypnotized. Therefore, we will not waste any further time trying to convince you that you can be hypnotized."

The patient then described a case history that he and his wife had read about: Erickson treated an enuretic couple by having them kneel on their bed every night and deliberately urinate.

They then slept in the wet sheets. This, my patient felt, was "Ericksonian" therapy.

I began a long, rather rambling discussion of the value of the unconscious mind, during which the patient obviously relaxed, let his eyelids close, and appeared to have entered into a hypnotic trance. I did not challenge him regarding the depth of his trance. While I was talking, however, I began associating to the story of the enuretics, and I recalled Erickson's comment at the end of another story. He had said, "Do you want a surefire technique for living a long life? Wake up every morning! And, to ensure that you *will* wake up every morning, drink a lot of fluid before you go to sleep and you *have* to wake up—to go to the bathroom to urinate."

I told the patient this story and then suggested to him that he drink at least one quart of liquid an hour before he went to sleep each night, and that, over a period of two weeks, he push forward his time of going to sleep by a half an hour each night. He had been going to sleep at about 3 A.M. and awakening at about 11 A.M. I suggested that he start going to sleep at about two o'clock, one-thirty, one, and, finally, at midnight, when his wife went to sleep. I also told him not to lie in bed awake. The bed must be associated with sleep or with lovemaking. If he was awake he must leave the bed, go into the living room, and read or watch television. Then he was to drink at least a quart of liquid before he went to sleep. This, I assured him, would cause his bladder to become full in six to eight hours and he would *have* to get out of bed, in order to urinate.

After he urinated, he was to take a shower, terminating with cold water, if possible. Then he was to dress, have breakfast, and proceed to work without ever returning to bed.

The patient objected that he did not like to take showers in the morning and usually took them at night. I insisted, again, that he was to take them in the morning—at least until he had overcome his waking-up problem. He promised he would do this and would call me in two or three weeks to let me know how this plan had worked. Two weeks later he called to report that he was having no problem with sleeping or waking.

The next day, I saw a sophisticated and intelligent woman who had initially contacted me for help in dealing with a painfully inflamed bladder, as well as sleep problems. At the beginning of the session I was not consciously thinking about her bladder difficulties. I knew that she had appeared in court the preceding week to finalize her divorce proceedings, but she appeared quite calm and pleasant as she entered my office. I know she was interested in Erickson's therapeutic approaches and told her about my experience with the Hasidic Jew.

I told her the story about my having advised him to drink the water before going to sleep, and I ended by adding Erickson's final comment when he had told the story. This was "We all begin to die from the moment we are born. Some do it faster than others. All we can do is enjoy our lives."

My patient began to weep copiously. I asked her if she wanted to tell me why she was weeping. (I wondered whether it was connected with the association to her urinary problems and my talk about urination.) She said that the talk about death had made her feel that her life was finished. This conviction had been building for some time. She felt that in spite of her professional success, and in spite of the fact that she had successfully raised two children, she no longer had any reason for living.

She related this feeling to the fact that her parents had never divorced, although they had separated when she was about eleven years old. Her mother forbade her to have anything to do with her father. This would be seen as a sign of disloyalty to the mother. Therefore, the patient felt that she had been denied a relationship with her father. She felt that if her parents had divorced she would have been free to see her father. Her father would have been free to have visitation rights and so on, and they would have had a relationship. Thus, she associated her divorce with freeing her own children. At the same time, she felt that her life was finished, now that she had completed this act.

This made me think of another story, which I then told her. I had had a dream after my first visit with Erickson. In the dream I had seen the words "You never finish anything." Seven years later, while I was listening to some Erickson tapes in Phoenix, I had an insight: "Who says that you have to finish anything? Nothing is ever really finished as long as we are alive."

I told the patient this story and suggested that perhaps she could conceive of her life as a continuation of the life of her parents, and of her children's life as a continuation of her life. And the process would continue as long as there was human life on earth. She found this thought comforting.

The main point of this rather long summary of two therapeutic hours with two different patients is that my selection of stories was not determined by any preconceived notions but arose from my own free associations, which were influenced by my life experiences, refined by more than thirty years of clinical experience. It is also important to emphasize that the process took place in the context of a good therapeutic relationship.

The patients selected parts that applied to themselves. They were not necessarily parts that I thought they might have selected. But they were helpful.

The danger in using these tales, as in the use of imagination in general, is that the imaginary experience can become a substitute for real-life experience. If one felt that he had already succeeded in satisfying life's needs, there would be no need for getting out of bed in the morning. Of course, when a therapist espouses a philosophy of activism, as Erickson did, he would never encourage a "do-nothing" type of existence. Those who listen to his stories are not likely to withdraw from life.

Sometimes my patients will note that even though they have an exciting session in the therapist's office, fantasizing and even imagining successful resolutions of conflicts, there is no carry-over. They complain that "there hasn't been any change in me. I am still not doing anything differently outside this office." Sometimes in such cases, it is best for the patient to remain silent and passive while I tell an Ericksonian tale. It may be a long, boring tale of childhood development. The patient will claim, at the end of the session, that this session was not as "good" as previous sessions and will state that he prefers to be more active. He may say that he was bored. I will remind him that the work that we are trying to achieve is on an unconscious level and that it does not matter what his conscious mind does. Subsequently, he may report major changes in his life. He has been, for example, more assertive socially, has established new relationships, or has changed a job. In other words, his activity takes place *outside* of the session. During the session, *I* assume responsibility for activity.

Of course, some patients may resent being told a story that was created by someone other than their own therapist. They may prefer a more personalized approach. Books, such as *Therapeutic Metaphors*, by David Gordon, inspired by Erickson's use of metaphors, provide help for those who would like to use Erickson's general approach while creating their own metaphors.

Obviously, the mere reading or telling of one or more of these tales is not likely to result in a transformation. Transformation is more likely to occur when the recipient, and perhaps the transmitter (as I will call the therapist), is in a receptive state. As previously mentioned, this receptive state is often most easily and quickly achieved by the inducing of a hypnotic trance. The optimal therapeutic relationship is not what is often called "positive transference." Rather, it is one in which there is a state of "rapport" between therapist and patient. Then, the unconscious mind of the patient and the therapist are most fully responsive to one another. If one reads these stories in the so-called waking state, one might dismiss them as being "clichéd," "corny," or "of interest, but not enlightening." Yet, in the hypnotic state, where everything that is said by the therapist is heightened in meaning, a story, or a single word in a story, may trigger a mini *satori*—the Zen term for enlightenment.

2. Motivating Tales

Erickson often used descriptions of earliest childhood development—learning to recognize one's own hand, learning to stand, to walk, and to talk—as a way of building a person's sense of his own process and growth. When he told me stories in which I was directed back to my earliest learnings, I was able—in the trance state—to reexperience the immense effort and frequent frustration involved in learning any new task or skill. At the same time, I was perfectly aware that I had learned these skills successfully. The implication was that I could learn to overcome other challenges in my present life.

As Jay Haley points out in Uncommon Therapy, Erickson had a clear-cut view of normal development. This does not mean that he tried to fit all individuals into the same pattern, but rather he believed that there was a normal, healthy core to each individual, perhaps something akin to what Horney called the "real self." He was aware of the many ways in which growth and development could be distorted and misdirected, but he felt that it was the therapist's task to bring the individual back to his own "real road."

Along this line, he told a story about a horse that wandered into his family's yard when he was a young man. The horse had no identifying marks. Erickson offered to return the horse to its owners. In order to accomplish this, he simply mounted the horse, led it to the road, and let the horse decide which way it wanted to go. He intervened only when the horse left the road to graze or wander into a field. When the horse finally arrived at the yard *of a neighbor several miles down the road, the neighbor asked Erickson, "How did you know that that horse came from here and was our horse?"*

Erickson said, "I didn't know—but the horse knew. All I did was to keep him on the road."

In beginning a course of therapy or of teaching, it is often helpful to go back to the beginning of the real road. An example of this occurs in the Erickson teaching tale "Learning to Stand Up."

LEARNING TO STAND UP

We learn so much at a conscious level and then we forget what we learn and use the skill. You see, I had a terrific advantage over others. I had polio, and I was totally paralyzed, and the inflammation was so great that I had a sensory paralysis too. I could move my eyes and my hearing was undisturbed. I got very lonesome lying in bed, unable to move anything except my eyeballs. I was quarantined on the farm with seven sisters, one brother, two parents, and a practical nurse. And how could I entertain myself? I started watching people and my environment. I soon learned that my sisters could say "no" when they meant "yes." And they could say "yes" and mean "no" at the same time. They could offer another sister an apple and hold it back. And I began studying nonverbal language and body language.

I had a baby sister who had begun to learn to creep. *I* would have to learn to stand up and walk. And you can imagine the intensity with which I watched as my baby sister grew from creeping to learning how to stand up. And you don't know how *you* learned how to stand up. You don't even know how you walked. You can *think* that you can walk in a straight line six blocks—with no pedestrian or vehicular traffic. You don't know that you *couldn't* walk in a straight line at a steady pace!

You don't know what you do when you walk. You don't know how you learned to stand up. You learned by reaching up your hand and pulling yourself up. That put pressure on your hands—and, by accident, you discovered that you could put weight on your *feet*. That's an awfully complicated thing because your knees would give way—and, when your knees would keep straight, your hips would give way. Then you got your feet crossed. And you couldn't stand up because both your knees and your hips would give way. Your feet were crossed—and you soon learned to get a wide brace—and you pull yourself up and you have the job of learning how to keep your knees straight—one at a time and as soon as you learn that, you have to learn how to give your attention to keep your hips straight. Then you found out that you had to learn to give your attention to keep your hips straight and knees straight at the same time *and* feet far apart! Now finally you could stand having your feet far apart, resting on your hands.

Then came the lesson in three stages. You distribute your weight on your one hand and your two feet, this hand not supporting you at all [E. raises his left hand]. Honestly hard work—allowing you to learn to stand up straight, your hips straight, knees straight, feet far apart, this hand [right hand] pressing down hard. Then you discover how to alter your body balance. You alter your body balance by turning your head, turning your body. You have to learn to coordinate all alterations of your body balance when you move your hand, your head, your shoulder, your body—and then you have to learn it all over again with the other hand. Then comes the terribly hard job of learning to have *both* hands up and moving your hands in all directions and to depend upon the two solid bases of your feet, far apart. And keeping your hips straight —your knees straight and keeping your mind's attention so divided that you can attend to your knees, your hips, your left arm, your right arm, your head, your body. And finally, when you had enough skill, you tried balancing on one foot. That was a hell of a job!

How do you hold your entire body keeping your hips straight, your knees straight and feeling hand movement, head movement, body movement? And then you put your one foot ahead and alter your body's center of gravity! Your knees bent—and you sat down! You got up again and tried it again. Finally you learned how to move one foot ahead and took a step and it seemed to be good. So you repeated it—it seemed so good. Then the third step —with the same foot—and you toppled! It took you a long time to alternate right left, right left, right left. Now you could swing your arms, turn your head, look right and left, and walk along, never paying a bit of attention to keeping your knees straight, hips straight.

Erickson is suggesting that a disability may give one an advantage, a "terrific advantage over others." He suggests that learning is one of the best forms of entertainment. When he is completely paralyzed he asks, "How can I entertain myself?" He follows that by describing how he developed his powers of observation. Then he tells about the pleasure of further learning—learning the things that are ordinarily unconscious—and gives the example of our unconscious actions and movements as we walk down the street.

When he talks about the actual process of learning to stand up, there is much emphasis on kinesthetic awareness, and the listener is likely to focus on his own inner kinesthetic sense. The clumsiness of trying to stand, accompanied by having feet crossed and so on, is like the clumsiness we all experience in trying to learn something new.

By describing plausible experiences that an infant might have in learning to stand and walk, he encourages regression of the listener to the infant level. In fact, nearly everyone, on listening to this story, will go into a hypnotic trance, with regression. The emphasis in the story is on learning a basic skill, consciously at first, and having it become unconscious. When the story is used

as a hypnotic induction, it encourages regression and the manifes-
tation of automatisms. It is interesting to note that Erickson's
negative statements (i.e., "you toppled") are in the past tense. He
changes to the present tense to imbed positive suggestions ("you
alter your body balance").

This "very early learning set" story is helpful at the beginning
of any therapeutic program because it brings the patient back to
a time before the onset of his neurotic problems, disrupting, at
least temporarily, his fixed mental sets. It also reminds the patient
that learning is or was difficult but that he will learn, if he persists.
After all, he knows that he can now walk, without effort.

Erickson is also pointing out that we have laid down the basic
building blocks and we will carry these basic building blocks with
us into the future. As a farm boy, Erickson was always concerned
with planting for a harvest that would be reaped in the future. In
this story, Erickson is laying down one of the building blocks for
therapy, by talking about how people learn. He is making the
learning process nonthreatening and interesting. He is also starting to illustrate some of the points that he will make over and over
again with other stories, that is, he watched things very closely.
He learned by watching others. He is cueing in the message "You
are here to learn," and he is stimulating a "learning set"—an
openness to learning. Paralysis is disabling, and a patient is involved with things that are disabling. Erickson turns this paralysis
into something useful. He was alone and could rely on nobody but
himself, and he started watching.

When he says that his sister could offer another sister an apple
and hold it back, is he saying that he can offer an apple—learning
—and hold it back? Or that you, yourself, can offer something of
yourself and still be holding some of it back? He is not offering
one or another message, but actually a multileveled message. And
the apple brings to mind the Garden of Eden—the beginning,
the genesis.

"And you can imagine the intensity with which I watched."
Here he is marking the word "imagine." Of course, this is the way
his hypnotic work will be done, with imagery, with imagining. He
is also starting the induction and focusing the listener's attention.

Jeff Zeig's comment on this story was, "Erickson had the
ability to play with your attention and to play with his own
attention. He chuckled his way through all of his stories. He was
going to have fun, and he was inviting you to play. If you did not
want to play, that was your problem. He would still make invita-
tions, but he was not going to be offended if you rejected them.
We still have scratched only the surface. I feel that I have a pretty
good understanding of Erickson's process, yet, if we sat down with
him to discuss what he was doing, we would discover we had hit
only the surface level, or perhaps one layer below the surface. He
would have in mind two more layers below the surface. He could
see those two or three layers when he presented the symbol of an
apple. It would be 'What does a little child think of an apple?'
or 'What do you do with an apple as a little child?' You bring an
apple to the teacher. And it was a symbol of being pleasing.
Erickson had an understanding of people's unconscious, so that
he would know that if you presented this type of word or symbol,
you could expect these possible associations. As you watched the
person, you could then grab on to whichever associations that
particular person had, and you could follow up on them. This kind
of depth is really unmatched. So you don't know how you learned
to stand up. But you have that information."

This was one of Erickson's important principles—that people
have, in their own natural history, the resources to overcome the
problem for which they are seeking help. In this story, he reminds
people that they have resources of which they are not yet aware.

When he uses phrases such as "You put pressure on your hand
—and by accident you discovered that you could put weight on
your feet," this was his way of conveying his idea of using "pro-

grammed accidents" in therapy. You put the patient into a situation and he is bound to discover things—if he is aware at all.

"It is an awfully complicated thing because your knees would give way and when your knees would keep straight, your hips would give way." He is cueing the unconscious with words such as "straight" and "stand up." Later, when these words or phrases are introduced into therapy, the entire learning set and attitude toward learning are then automatically evoked.

THE BOY WILL BE DEAD BY MORNING

I graduated from high school in June 1919. In August, I heard three doctors, in the other room, tell my mother, "The boy will be dead by morning." [Erickson had his first poliomyelitis infection at age seventeen.]

Being a normal kid, I resented that.

Our country doctor had called in two Chicago men, as consultants, and they told my mother, "The boy will be dead by morning."

I was infuriated. The idea of telling a mother that her son would be dead by morning! It's outrageous!

Afterwards, my mother came into my room, bland of face. She thought I was delirious, because I insisted that she move the large chest in my room, in order for it to be at a different angle beside the bed. She put it beside the bed one way and I kept telling her to move it back and forth, until I was satisfied. That chest was blocking my view through the window—and I was damned if I would die without seeing the sunset! I only saw half of it. I was unconscious for three days.

I didn't tell my mother. She didn't tell me.

Erickson told me this touching story in 1970, when I had come to him asking for help in improving my memory for names and in recovering childhood memories. I immediately recalled some childhood memories—of my own bout with a serious febrile illness, scarlet fever. But my desire for a better memory for names was not to be fulfilled. It was only later that I realized that he was indirectly suggesting that I accept this limitation. His suggestion was also conveyed in a story about his father's comment at his mother's funeral.

"And, at my mother's funeral, my father remarked, 'It was nice to have seventy-four wedding anniversaries with one person. It would have been nicer to have seventy-five, but you can't have everything.' "

Through that story and also through the preceding one, he is telling us, indirectly, that we are lucky to be alive.

In his reference to the chest and the sunset, he was also conveying one of his favorite prescriptions for enjoying life, perhaps even for prolonging it! "Always look to a real goal, in the near future." In this case, his goal was to see the sunset. Of course, before this goal could be achieved, it was necessary to move the obstacle. Since Erickson could not do this himself, he needed to get his mother to do it. Significantly, he didn't tell her why he wanted the chest moved. It is not always necessary for us to give reasons for our actions. But it is necessary that we have goals— immediate and achievable.

DILATATION

Erickson never made miraculous claims for hypnosis. Still, he noted repeatedly that we all possess powers, natural powers, that we do not utilize. With appropriate motivating suggestions and direction, these powers can often be harnessed and used. When he told the following story, in response to the question "Is hypnosis helpful in the treatment of cancer?" he was referring mainly to its value in the alleviation of pain. There was some implication *that along with such conventional treatments as surgery, hypnosis might improve the patient's chances of survival.*

I think a great deal can be done. The president of the state medical society, a surgeon, sent me a woman. He had operated on her for cancer of the uterus and then operated on her for cancer of the colon, of a different variety.

She developed a contraction of the lower colon. Defecation was extremely painful, and she went to his office for slow, gradual dilatation. And she suffered from such terrible pain. He asked me, "Can you help the woman with hypnosis? I don't want to do a third operation on that woman."

So I used a trance. I told the woman that she had had two cancers of different kinds; now she suffered from a painful contraction of the lower colon. And that's very painful and had to be dilated. I told her that if, every day, she would get into her swimming suit, throw an automobile tire into the swimming pool, sit in there, and enjoy the comfort of the swimming pool and the water, the dilatation would be much less painful.

And she did that every day. The doctor said the dilatation proceeded much more rapidly, unusually rapidly. He said the woman complained about pain as before, but the tone of her voice was different. He didn't think she had the same degree of pain.

About a year later the woman came by and hugged and kissed me and told me how wonderful life was. Her colon had healed; the doctor said she had a normal colon. He had removed the cancer from it. No recurrence.

Erickson is suggesting that "dilatation" will be much less painful if a person takes some action—getting a tire tube and then sitting in the swimming pool, in comfort. He is setting the mood for the therapy that will follow, suggesting that it could be done in relative comfort. He is also suggesting that it will "proceed

much more rapidly, unusually rapidly." The final implication is
that the therapy will be successful, as it was with this woman, in
spite of the fact that she was suffering from a condition that is
often fatal. Since instructions, in this case, a rather homey remedy
for pain, are given in hypnosis, they would have more power than
if they were given in the waking state.

Erickson might tell this type of story to convey a message to
someone in the group who he felt was emotionally or mentally
"constipated." He might indicate that the message was intended
for that particular person by looking in one direction and directing his voice in another, or by changing the tone of his voice when
he was facing that particular person, or by avoiding looking at that
particular person.

QUARRELING

A man from Philadelphia, whose headaches I cured, sent his
aunt and uncle out to see me. He said, "Those two have quarreled
every day of their married life. They've been married over thirty
years."

They came out to see me. I said, "Haven't you had enough
of quarreling? Why not start enjoying life?" And they had a very
pleasant life. And the man's aunt tried to persuade her sister to
come out, because his mother was very unhappy.

In this story, Erickson, in the indirect manner that is typical
of him, is answering critics who ask about follow-up on his patients. He makes it clear that the headache cure was effective by
telling us that "the man from Philadelphia" sent his aunt and
uncle to see him. It is also obvious that their situation was improved since the aunt felt Erickson could help her sister. Erickson
often begins a case report with reference to a previous patient who
was treated successfully.

This story might be told by Erickson when someone in the group was arguing inwardly with him or with himself. He marks the phrase "Haven't you had enough of quarreling?"

The story may be difficult to believe. I present it, however, because its simplicity is so appealing.

I asked Erickson to tell us more about the context in which these simple suggestions had been given. How much time had he spent in establishing rapport? Did he hypnotize the couple?

He said, "I just used a waking trance which developed into a light trance. I asked them, 'But why not enjoy life? You've had over thirty years of quarreling. I think marriage should be enjoyable. And you haven't too many years left to enjoy marriage.' And they were appreciative.

"Too many therapists think that they must direct the change and help the patient to change. Therapy is like starting a snowball rolling at the top of a mountain. As it rolls down, it grows larger and larger and becomes an avalanche that fits the shape of the mountain."

3. Trust the Unconscious

I'D LEARNED MUCH

At Oswego College in New York, Estabrooks [a professor of psychiatry] said, when I went up to him, "I'll schedule you to give a convocation for teachers this evening." There would be a lot of townspeople attending and I had a lot of things to do before I went to the auditorium, unrelated to the lecture. I was not concerned, however, because I knew I could talk and I knew I could think and I knew that I'd learned much in the course of the years.

In the above vignette, and the two that follow, Erickson models an attitude of trust in one's long-term memories and in unconsciously stored knowledge. He underlines the fact that the unconscious mind is a repository of memories and skills that can be called upon after many years. He was fond of quoting Will Rogers, "It ain't what we don't know that gives us trouble. It's what we know that ain't so that gives us trouble." To which Erickson would add, "The things that we know, but don't know we know, give us even more trouble."

LIGHT SNOW

In the village of Lowell, Wisconsin, it snowed for the first time that autumn on November 12, shortly before 4:00 P.M. And that kid in the third seat, in the third row of seats, right beside the window, wondered, How long will I remember this?

I was just wondering. . . .

I knew exactly . . . I knew it was November 12, in the year 1912. It was a very light snow.

NARWHAL

On the farm we had two books—the history of the United States and an unabridged dictionary. I read that dictionary from A to Z, repeatedly. And I had a tremendous vocabulary. Much later, while I was lecturing in Montana, a doctor invited me to spend an evening at his home. During the course of the evening he brought out a very peculiar spiral-shaped object and asked, "Do you know what that is?"

I said, "Yes, it's a narwhal tusk."

He said, "You're the first person who has even looked at that and recognized it. My grandfather was a whaler and he got this tusk from a narwhal. It has been in the family. And I have always been very quiet about it. I let people examine it and wonder and wonder and wonder. Now, how did you know it was a narwhal tusk?"

I said, "When I was five or six years old, I saw a picture of it in an unabridged dictionary."

HE WILL TALK

A lot of people were worried because I was four years old and didn't talk, and I had a sister two years younger than me who talked, and she is still talking but she hasn't said anything. And many people got distressed because I was a four-year-old boy who couldn't talk.

My mother said, comfortably, "When the time arrives, then he will talk."

This last tale highlights Erickson's belief that the unconscious mind can be trusted to produce appropriate responses at the right time. When this story is told to a patient who is just beginning to experience hypnotic trance, it may encourage him to wait patiently until the urge to talk arises or until he is able to reveal unconscious messages in a nonverbal way.

SCRATCHING HOGS

One summer I sold books to pay my way through college. I walked into a farmyard about five o'clock, interviewed the farmer about buying books, and he said, "Young fellow, I don't read anything. I don't need to read anything. I'm just interested in my hogs."

"While you're busy feeding the hogs, do you mind if I stand and talk to you?" I asked.

He said, "No, talk away, young fellow, it won't do you a bit of good. I'm not going to pay attention to you; I am busy feeding the hogs."

And so I talked about my books. Being a farm boy, I thoughtlessly picked up a pair of shingles lying on the ground and started scratching the hogs' backs as I was talking. The farmer looked over, stopped, and said, "Anybody knows how to scratch a hog's back, the way hogs like it, is somebody I want to know. How about having supper with me tonight and you can sleep overnight with no charge and I will buy your books. *You like hogs.* You know how to scratch 'em the way they liked to be scratched."

Here, Erickson is recounting how he had unconsciously acted in precisely the best way to achieve his purpose—in this case, to sell books. He emphasizes the fact that he had "thoughtlessly" picked up some shingles and had scratched the hog's back as he was talking to the farmer. The farmer unconsciously responded to a man whom he felt to be a kindred soul.

Of course, Erickson is not teaching a way to sell books, or to manipulate people. He genuinely was able to relate to this farmer, partly because he too was a farm boy. The action that was effective—the scratching of the hog's back—could be expressed because Erickson was free in expressing himself. He is urging the listener to trust his own unconscious as he had trusted his unconscious and as the farmer had trusted his own unconscious in responding to the young Erickson.

This story also illustrates the principle that I have designated as "Join the Patient."

Erickson told me this story in August 1979, after I asked him why he chose me to write the Foreword to his book Hypnotherapy. Before he began his tale about scratching hogs he had answered, "I liked you and you gave a gold frog to my wife." (When I had first visited Erickson, in 1970, I was returning from Los Angeles to New York with a collection of live snakes, geckos, and frogs. I had given him a beautiful yellow frog as a gift.)

He elaborated, "You made a good impression on me. I liked you. You are genuine. You are honest. You are thoughtful. You are intelligent and you were willing to go from New York to San Francisco or L.A. just because you liked frogs! My impression in this room is—the guy likes carvings. That should be your impression of me. That guy really likes carvings. And there is more to him than sitting in a chair making dollars as a psychoanalyst. He's got other interests. And frogs are a far step from psychoanalysis and psychiatry, literature, and so on. You've got a wide breadth there."

At the conclusion of his tale he underlined his point by look-

*ing directly at me with his clearest and kindliest gaze and com-
menting, "I like the way you scratch a hog." He made it clear that
he trusted his unconscious in his selection of collaborators, just as
he did in other decisions.*

SEVEN ASTERISKS

One of my subjects was a most excellent person with whom
I did a lot of experimental work. He was a psychologist. He had
a master's degree and he was really undecided about his future.
We used him experimentally and he became aware that he had
an unconscious mind. I loaned him my medical books and he
entered medical school. In his senior year, one of his professors,
who liked him very much, said, "Arthur, how do you think you
will get along in my examination?" And Arthur replied, "I won't
have any trouble with your examination. You have only got ten
questions and they are—." And he proceeded to name all ten
questions.

The professor said, "Well, you know exactly the questions I'm
going to ask! You have even told them to me in the order that
I have got those questions. Did you break in to my office and get
hold of the carbon copy?"

Arthur said, "No, I just knew what you would ask on a final
examination."

The professor said, "That's not good enough for me. I'm
going to take you in to talk to the dean."

The dean listened to the story. He said, "Is that true, Arthur?
Do you know the questions?"

Arthur said, "Of course I know the questions. I attended his
course and I listened to his lectures."

And the dean said, "In some way you must have gotten hold
of the mimeographed sheet. Unless you can prove otherwise, I

will have to bar you from taking the examination, and you are not going to graduate, because of dishonesty."

Arthur said, "You want proof that I knew, before the professor did, what his questions were going to be. You could send someone to my room and get my notebook with the notes I took on his lectures. And you will notice that I have certain things marked with asterisks. All the questions that the professor is going to ask are marked with seven asterisks. You will see that '1' and '2' and '3' are variously applied to those 'asterisk questions.' Because he has a habit of asking only ten questions, I selected ten notes that I gave seven asterisks to, because those were the things he gave most emphasis to—both throughout the year and during the summary session at the end of the year."

Now, they sent someone to get that notebook and found that Arthur had marked some notes with one asterisk, some with two, some with three, some with four, some with five, some with six —and that there were only ten marked with seven asterisks. And the asterisks were numbered, not serially, from 1 to 10. The middle one was 1 and maybe the top one was 9 and so on.

Then the dean said, "You don't have to take the examination. You really listened and you heard the special intonation that the lecturer gave to those particular points."

When you listen to a lecturer, and you pay attention to the emphasis that he gives various topics, you can pick out the things that he is going to include in his examination. Arthur was remarkable; he had a remarkable sense of hearing and a remarkable sense of pitch, so he always knew in advance what topic would be included in the examination. The teacher would give it away. They tell you what is most important and they always want the importance to be recognized by the students. Now, sometimes they think a point that is not really important is important. Be careful to remember that point, because that will be included in the examination. Communication is a very complicated thing.

Our facial expression, our eyes, the way we hold our bodies, the way we move our bodies and our extremities, the way we move our heads and so on, the way we move certain individual muscles —all this discloses a lot of information.

In this story the young psychologist–medical student had learned not only to trust his unconscious mind but also to develop his perceptive skills to a rather extreme degree. As Erickson said, "Arthur was remarkable." Of course, most of us have not developed our perceptual skills to such an extent. Still, if we know that it is possible, we may be encouraged in a similar direction, especially when we receive clear-cut messages in our dreams or in our associations.

The lecturer in this story is unconsciously signaling what he wanted his students to learn. Erickson is telling us to listen to these unconscious cues. In the story, the student was able to translate his unconscious awareness into consciousness. Listeners and readers can respond to Erickson's subliminal messages even without conscious awareness, however. In fact, he is instructing them to do so.

In the induction and utilization of trance, Erickson encourages us to strive for this same attitude—of trust in our unconscious mind. He does so in the following explanation to therapists:

You see, trance induction should not be a laborious thing. The mere confidence in your own voice. The mere confidence in your ability to induce a trance is the most important thing of all. And anybody who is human is going to get into a trance—even very paranoid patients—if you are very careful. I don't advise a trance for paranoid patients, because they can become paranoid in the trance state too. But, experimentally, I have determined that all patients can go into a trance state—that *anybody* can.

Now, is it necessary to know that you are in a trance? No, it isn't. How deep a trance is necessary? Any trance that is of sufficient level to let your unconscious mind take a look, a mental look, at what's going on, is sufficient. In those mental looks and understandings, you learn a great deal more than you do by conscious effort. And you should use your mind at the unconscious level, even while you are using it at the conscious level.

CURIOUS

A woman came to college always holding her left hand over her mouth. She recited in class holding her left hand under her nose, concealing her mouth. She walked out on the street with her left hand covering her mouth. She ate in restaurants concealing her mouth behind her left hand. When she was reciting in class, walking down the street, eating in restaurants, always the left hand was over her mouth.

Now that interested me. I made it a point to get acquainted with her. She told me, after much prodding, about a horrible experience she had when she was ten years old. In a car accident, she had been thrown through a windshield. A frightening experience for a ten-year-old girl. Her mouth was cut by the windshield glass and there was a lot of blood on the hood of the car. A lot of blood that was frightening to a ten-year-old could be a very small amount of blood, but, to her, it was an enormous quantity. She grew up with the idea that her mouth was terribly scarred— and that's why she kept her mouth covered, because she did not want anybody to see that horrible scar.

I got her to read a history of cosmetology and she came across beauty spots—spots that were crescent shaped, circles, stars, and so on. She read about how a woman would place a beauty spot near the feature she considered attractive. I induced her to draw me some beauty spots. Then I induced her, in the privacy of her room, to make a life-size copy of her scar—it turned out to be a five-pointed star, the size of a beauty spot. Yet she still saw it as larger than her whole face.

So I persuaded her to go on a date with one of the students. She was to carry two heavy handbags in order to keep her hands down, from the face. On this date, and on subsequent ones, she discovered that if she allowed a good-night kiss, the man would invariably kiss her on the scarred side of her mouth. Even though she had two sides to her mouth the man would always, invariably, kiss her on the scarred side. She dated one man but didn't have the nerve to let him have a good-night kiss. The second man kissed her on the right side of her mouth. So did the next, the third, the fourth, the fifth, and the sixth. What she didn't know was that she was curious and when she was curious she always tipped her head to the left, so that a man had to kiss her on the right side of her mouth!

Every time I tell that case history, I look around. You all know about subliminal speech, but you don't know about subliminal hearing. When I tell that case history, every woman puckers her lips—and I know what she is thinking of. You watch the neighbor come in to see the new baby. You watch the lips. You know just when that neighbor is going to kiss the baby.

By noticing the direction in which the girl characteristically tilted her head when she was curious about something, Erickson was able to predict that she would tilt it in the same way when she was about to be kissed. He is teaching the importance of using the information that is unconsciously disclosed by the patient. Erickson helped her to discover what he had already discovered, that is, that she tilted her head when her curiosity was invoked. To help her make this discovery, he prevented her from using her usual defense mechanism, covering her scarred mouth with her left hand. She was then able to conclude, after several men had kissed her on the scarred side of her mouth, that it was not really ugly.

Erickson utilizes a trick that is well known to magicians. He directs our attention to one place when, actually, what is going on is someplace else. For example, he tempts us to think about "Why is she covering her mouth with her left hand?" Actually, this is not important. He is observing the way she tilts her head, and that is important.

PROFESSOR RODRIGUEZ

I go into trances so that I will be more sensitive to the intonations and inflections of my patients' speech. And to enable me to hear better, see better. I go into a trance and forget the presence of others. And people *see* me in a trance.

There was a patient, Rodriguez, a professor of psychiatry from Peru. He wrote tht he wanted psychotherapy from me. I knew him by reputation. I knew that he was far better educated than I was. I knew that he was quicker witted than I was. I regarded him as much more intelligent than I. And here he was, asking to come to be my patient.

I wondered, "How can I handle a man who is brighter, better educated, quicker witted than I am?" He was Castilian Spanish, and extremely arrogant—arrogant and ruthless, very insulting to deal with. I gave him a two o'clock appointment. I took down his name, address, his local address, his marital status, all the statistics. Then I looked up to ask him, "How do you see your problem?" The chair was empty.

I looked at the clock. It was not around two o'clock. It was four o'clock. I noticed that I had a manila folder with sheets of paper inside. So I realized that I had gone into a hypnotic trance to interview him.

Then one day after twelve or fourteen hours of therapy, Rodriguez jumped to his feet and said, "Dr. Erickson, you're in a trance!"

I awakened and said, "I know you're brighter than I am and more intelligent, quicker witted, much better educated. And that you are very arrogant. I didn't feel I could handle you and I wondered how I would handle you. I didn't know until after the first interview that my unconscious mind decided to take over the job. I know I've got sheets, notes, in the folder. I haven't read them yet. And I will read them, now, after you leave."

Rodriguez looked at me angrily and said (pointing to a photograph), "Are those your parents?"

I said, "Yes."

He said, "Your father's occupation?"

I said, "He's a retired farmer."

And Rodriguez said, scornfully, "Peasants!"

Now I knew that he knew a lot of history. I said, "Yes, peasants. And, for all I know, the blood of the bastards of my ancestors runs in *your* veins." He knew about the Vikings overrunning all of Europe. He was a good boy after that. Now that took a bit of rapid thinking, to get "the blood of the bastards of my ancestors may run in your veins."

I knew Rodriguez had left England without paying Ernest Jones his fee for his psychoanalysis. I knew he had left Duke University with a lot of debts behind him. And, as we began the last week, I had Rodriguez give me the names of all the important people he knew. I put down their addresses. He was very pleased to show off that way. I got them all written down and then I said, "Are you going to pay by check or cash?"

He said, "You tricked me."

I said, "I thought it was necessary. I earned my fee."

So I got my fee. Why else would I want to know the names

and addresses of all his important friends? He knew blackmail when he heard it.

This was one of Erickson's favorite stories to illustrate the value of trance for a therapist, in order to enable him to find the best ways of responding effectively to his patients. This story requires little comment. It does emphasize the importance of the therapist's being "one up" when he is dealing with an arrogant patient. Erickson builds up to this by first pointing out the ways in which he was actually inferior to Rodriguez. This makes his having the last word all the more effective. He is giving us a submessage. Even though we may feel "inferior" to another person, even though we may feel inadequate, if we will dig into our unconscious minds we can find resources to equalize situations or bring us to a superior position. We may have to dredge up our ancestors, as Erickson did, but that is all right. Erickson would certainly not deprive us of the assets and resources we have inherited. He believed in using whatever one has—all of one's resources.

HUEY DUCK, DEWEY DUCK, AND LOUIE DUCK

I had a very difficult paragraph to write. I kept trying and trying, ending up in a blind alley. And one day I said, "Well, I have two hours before my next patient comes in. I think I will lean back and go into a trance and see what my unconscious has to say about that difficult paragraph."

I waited until about fifteen minutes before that patient came in and I was surprised to see, in my lap, a box of comic books belonging to the kids. There were two stacks of comic books on my desk. The patient was due so I put the comic books back in the box, went out into the other room, and saw my patient.

A couple of weeks later I thought, "Well, I haven't gotten the answer to that paragraph yet." I had a little time to spare and I took a pencil and something came to my mind immediately: "And Donald Duck said to Huey Duck, Dewey Duck, and Louie Duck . . ." and I thought with amusement that Donald Duck comic books appealed to the intelligence of the adult as well as the youthful. They have to be succinct, clear, and subtle. So I wrote the paragraph. My unconscious knew where to get an example.

Here is another story that emphasizes the value of the unconscious as a problem solver. Erickson told me this story after I asked him for help in scheduling patients and with writing. Obviously, what he was saying to me was that I ought to go into a trance, giving myself an adequate amount of time, as he had, and that I should then listen to my unconscious mind. Subsequently, I followed this advice and found several solutions. Once, when I experienced a writing block, I entered into a self-hypnotic trance after asking myself, "How could I overcome this block?" I noted a tingling feeling on the inside of my right thumb, on the lateral side of my middle finger, and on the medial side of my index finger. I soon understood that these tingling feelings were located in the exact locations where a pen would make contact. My unconscious message was that I should begin writing by hand, and then switch to dictation. I did this and overcame the writing block.

WALKING DOWN THE STREET

You, at your present age, walk down the street, you try to walk in a straight line at a steady pace, and you happen to be hungry and you automatically slow down when you pass the first restaurant. If you are a woman you may automatically veer towards a jeweler's window. If you are a sportsman you automatically veer towards a sporting-goods-store window. If you have been neglecting your teeth and you know you should get a dental appointment and don't care for that, you automatically speed up when you pass a dental building.

I took up a station where I could watch young women walking past a medical building. When they altered their gait in a certain way, slowed down, and their arm swinging altered and a very soft expression came over their faces as they walked past the medical building, I would cross over and ask, "Was the first frog test or rabbit test positive?" Unthinkingly, they would say, "The first one was, or I hope it will be."

One young woman altered her walk, arm swing, and facial expression. You could see a fear reaction! You have to be careful —she is not married!

Every person, old or young, male or female, automatically slows down as if the air had become thick and difficult to penetrate. Do you know at what building?—a bakery! That powerful olfactory stimulus slows you automatically.

Again, we are given an example illustrating that most of our behavior is unconsciously determined. Erickson is also inserting frequent references to "automatic" behavior. Thus, this tale is useful in encouraging a patient to allow himself to respond automatically in a hypnotic trance. The repetition in the story can easily lead to a hypnotic trance, especially if the words are delivered in a rhythmic way.

Of course, this story can be used diagnostically as well. One can note a patient's response as one mentions the various elements in the story—the jeweler, the sporting-goods store, the dental building. Concerns about pregnancy may emerge in response to the part that refers to a young woman's concern about being pregnant. The commentary about the bakery may very easily bring a subject back to early childhood memories that are associated with the smells of baking or cooking.

I wondered why Erickson emphasized the fact that "every person . . . slows down automatically" when passing a bakery. I finally realized that the message he was giving me was "Slow down, Rosen." He is telling all of his listeners to slow down and allow time for learning and for sensory associations.

AUTOMATIC WRITING

Every little movement should be regarded. Many times, by writing "yes," questions can be answered. A girl may ask, "Am I really in love?" and I will ask, "Who do you think you are in love with?"

"Oh, there is Bill, Jim and Pete and George."

Then I ask, "Is it Bill?"

She writes, "Yes."

"Is it George?"

"Yes."

"Is it Jim?"

"Yes."

"Is it Pete?"

"Yes."

But if the "yes" causes a hole and the hole is punched in the paper by heaviness of the pencil, that's *really* the boy. Yet, she still doesn't want to know.

Once at Michigan State University, Dr. Anderson gave a lecture on hypnosis to the psychology department—to the entire department. Dr. Anderson asked me if I wanted to demonstrate. I said I had no subject and I would appreciate some volunteers. A number of students were called and asked if they would like to volunteer, and quite a number volunteered. I picked a girl named Peggy. One of the things that Dr. Anderson wanted was automatic writing. I had Peggy go to the far end of a long table; and all the rest of us went to the other end of the table.

I put Peggy into a trance. She was aware that we were sitting at the far end of the long table and that she was at the other end. She wrote something automatically. Then she automatically folded her paper, folded it again, and automatically slipped it into her handbag. She didn't notice any of that. All the rest of us did. I put her back in a trance and told her that after she awakened, she would automatically write, "It's a beautiful day in June." It was April.

She wrote that and after I showed it to her she said that she didn't write it and that it wasn't her handwriting. It certainly wasn't her handwriting.

The following September she called me long distance from Indiana and said, "A funny thing happened today, and I think you're connected with it—so I'll tell you what it is. I emptied my handbag today. I found a wad of paper in it. I opened it and on one side was written, in a strange handwriting, 'Will I marry Harold?' It wasn't my handwriting. I don't know how that paper got into my handbag. And I have a feeling you're connected with it. And my only connection with you is that lecture you gave in April at Michigan State University. Do you have any explanation of that piece of paper?"

I said, "I lectured at the university in April; that's true. Now, were you by chance engaged to get married to anybody then?"

"Oh yes, I was engaged to Bill."

I said, "Did you have any doubts about your engagement then?"

"No, I didn't."

"Did you ever develop doubts about your engagement to Bill?"

"Oh, last June, Bill and I broke up."

"What has happened since then?"

"Oh, in July, I married a man named Harold."

"How long had you known Harold?"

"Oh, I knew him, by sight, during some part of the second semester but had never met him, never talked to him. I didn't, till I happened to meet him by chance, in July."

I said, "That handwriting 'Will I marry Harold?' was written by you, automatically, in a trance state. Your unconscious mind already recognized that you were going to break off with Bill and that Harold was the man who really appealed to you." Her unconscious knew, months in advance, that she would break her engagement. The reason she folded it up was that, consciously, she couldn't stand facing that fact in April.

With the first automatic handwriting you have a patient do, unless you make it very obvious that they are protected, they will have difficulty in writing freely, because something personal to the self is coming forth and they are not yet ready to face it. So if you want to use automatic writing, let your patient say, "I can't," and teach him to let the hand move in a scrawl. Gradually, after a number of scrawls, he will put secret information into a scrawl that can't be read. Then he will write other things like "This is a beautiful day in June." Then he can branch out and yield personal information. I once spent sixteen hours deciphering, very slowly, some illegible handwriting that eventually told a whole story—I think that is in "The Collected Papers."*

The very pressure of handwriting can convey an important message. It was serendipitous that Erickson suggested to Peggy that she write the phrase "It is a beautiful day in June." June was

---

*Advanced Techniques in Hypnosis and Psychotherapy, ed. Jay Haley (New York: Grune and Stratton, 1967).

the month in which she broke up with her fiancé, Bill. And, of course, June is the month we associate with weddings.

TRANCES IN BALI

When Margaret Mead, Jane Belo, and Gregory Bateson went to Bali in 1937, they went for the purpose of studying autohypnosis in the Balinese culture. In the Balinese culture, you could be going to a market. On the way to the market the Balinese can go into a deep trance, do their shopping, turn around, and come out of the trance when they get home—or stay in the trance and visit with a neighbor who is not in a trance, while they are in a trance. Autohypnosis is part of their daily life. Mead, Bateson, and Belo studied their behavior and brought back movies for me to examine. Dr. Mead wanted to know if a Balinese trance and the trance of the Occident were the same. Now, she [Lucy, a student] made the body-orientation movements that the Balinese people do, closing her hands, wanting to stand on her toes, getting reacquainted with the body. It is characteristic of a trance.

This story demonstrates that it is possible to carry out ordinary activities, such as shopping and visiting with neighbors, while one is in a trance state. It is not necessary to carry out unusual behavior. At the end of the story, Erickson relates the Balinese trance experience to that in the West by pointing out that the body-orientation movements of a therapist (Lucy) in his office are similar to those of the Balinese people when they come out of a trance. With this example, which is set in a distant and, for most of us, exotic place, Erickson is conveying two messages. The first is that trance is a rather ordinary experience, experienced by all of us. The second is that trance is somewhat exotic and glamorous.

4. Indirect Suggestion

The tales in this chapter demonstrate Erickson's application of "traditional" hypnotic phenomena, such as literalness, age regression, and distortions of time and space. They also illustrate his unique contribution to hypnotherapy, that is, the use of indirect suggestions. His indirect approach is especially useful in dealing with what is usually called "resistance" to hypnosis and to therapy. For example, in the tale "Walking Around the Resistance," the reality of hypnotic trance is indirectly suggested to a doubting, demanding doctor when he is confronted with another subject, who was, obviously, in a trance. For a comprehensive discussion of indirect suggestion the reader is referred to Hypnotherapy, *by Erickson and Rossi.*

THE HYPNOTIC SUBJECT IS LITERAL

I had a girl over for a demonstration of deep trance and trance phenomena for Dr. Ernest Rossi. I told her to go into a deep trance and to meet me in the middle of nowhere. She promptly opened her eyes, in the trance state, and said, very earnestly, "There is something awfully wrong!"

Dr. Rossi did not know what was wrong—but she knew what was wrong. Now, what's wrong about meeting me in the middle of nowhere?

There *is* no middle of nowhere! It's vacant space.

I had her close her eyes and I awakened her from the trance, and then I said, "I want you to do another task for me. I want you to meet me in outer space after going into a trance."

She opened her eyes in a trance state. It was obvious that she was not oriented to the room, the floor, or anything. Then I told her, "See this paperweight in my hand. Now, put that paperweight into a different position."

What did she do? She said, "Dr. Erickson, there are only three positions. I am in one, you are in one, the paperweight is in the third. Those are the *only* positions."

The hypnotic subject listens very literally.

I had her awaken again and I told her a shaggy-dog joke. "The cowboy was out riding one day and he came to a mountain, so high that it took him two looks to see to the top. He looked upwards as far as he could. Then he took a second look beginning where the first look left off." I put her into a trance and told her, "When you open your eyes I want you to see my hands, but not beyond them. Now lean forward and look."

She said, "Pink and gray. Those are your hands, Dr. Erickson, but where are you? I see your hands but you do not have any wrists. And, Dr. Erickson, there is something awfully wrong that I am seeing. Your hands are two-dimensional and I know they should be three-dimensional."

Now, when we deal with hypnosis, bear in mind that the unconscious places very specific meanings upon words. All your lives you have been learning things, transferring that knowledge to your unconscious and using, automatically, the end results of the learning. You learned to talk and there was a time when you thought "dink-a-wa-wa" was a drink of water. It took you a long time to discover that "dink-a-wa-wa" is not a drink of water; and that is why it takes a long time for patients, as adults, to understand, after you explain very carefully that "there is a language you don't understand—although you once did."

At the same time that Erickson is pointing up the fact that a hypnotic subject responds literally to suggestions, he is empha-sizing that unconscious learnings do not remain fixed, but are added to with new learning. "All your lives you have been learning things, transferring them to your unconscious, and using, auto-matically, the end results of the learning." He is suggesting that you, the reader, will transfer to your unconscious mind the learn-ings derived from his teaching tales and you will use the end result automatically.

ORANGES

One patient went to a drugstore with a prescription for one dose of castor oil. When she handed the druggist her prescription, she told him castor oil made her very sick. When she got home, she'd have to take the castor oil and get sick to her stomach.

So the druggist said, "While I'm preparing your dose of castor oil, would you like a glass of fresh orange juice?"

She noticed that the fresh orange juice tasted somewhat diff-erently. After she finished her glass, she said, "Now, for my prescription?"

The druggist said, "You've already taken it, in the orange juice."

Within a few days she noticed a billboard advertising Sunkist oranges; she got very sick to her stomach. She went into a restau-rant, saw some oranges, and got sick to her stomach. She couldn't go shopping for her mother if there were oranges in the store. And she had to discard a lot of her clothing that was orange in color. It got so that when she even *heard* the word "orange," she got very sick to her stomach, and that led to a severe headache.

I arranged that she be invited to a party at the hospital, as she was a friend of one of the doctors on the staff. I arranged things with that doctor friend. Subsequently, at the party, he demanded that I demonstrate hypnosis, so I hypnotized first this person, then that one. Finally, she volunteered as a hypnotic subject.

In the trance state I regressed her to the age of three years, long before the castor-oil episode. She was in a deep somnambulistic trance, having negative and positive hallucinations. The host asked everybody if they would like some orange juice. And everybody did want orange juice. So he brought in a basketful of oranges, squeezed them, and sat down beside the girl. We chatted about this topic and that. I had her see him, talk to him. And we all drank orange juice. Later I had her awaken with an undefinable taste in her mouth, but a good taste. As she went home that night she passed the billboard and said, "That's funny, that billboard doesn't make me sick any more."

And thereafter she drank orange juice and wore her orange dresses. Later, she recalled, "I can't remember just when the sight of oranges made me sick, but it doesn't any more. I wonder why it was? I can't remember when it was."

Just reorienting a person in time did that. If you were afraid of heights and you couldn't climb Squaw Peak, what would I do? I would disorient you in time, even if I have to go back ten or twelve years. You'd go out for a walk as if you were eighteen years younger, when you might not have had that phobia. So you'd climb that mountain, to see what's on the other side.

Or, if I couldn't do that with you, I would disorient your perception of things so that the mountain would look like flat land, a flat piece of land, like fresh sod that you can plough freshly. It is rough walking. You'd climb the mountain, and blame it on the plowing. It would get you over the mountain. Then I'd have you slowly recover your orientation.

On a warm summer's day, in your sleep, you can go skating on ice. And you can dine in New Orleans, San Francisco, or Honolulu. You can fly a plane, drive a car, meet all kinds of friends, and yet you're still sound asleep in bed.

You realize that every patient has had that sort of experience, so, in a trance state, you can suggest that a dream can turn into a feeling of hypnotic reality. A trance only allows you to handle all the learning you have already acquired. And we often disregard the learnings that we have acquired.

WALKING AROUND THE RESISTANCE

In this next tale Erickson demonstrates a very effective way of dealing with resistance to hypnosis.

The first time I practiced hypnosis in Phoenix, a doctor called me up and demanded an appointment. The tone of his voice warned me, "This is trouble. He's demanding that I put him in a trance." I gave him an appointment for the next day. He came into the office and said, "Now hypnotize me."

So I failed, by using a great number of techniques in ways to insure that they wouldn't work. Then I said, "Excuse me for a moment" and went out into the kitchen, where I had an Arizona State University coed working. And I said, "Ilse, I've got a very antagonistic, resistant patient in my office. I'm going to put you into a trance, a somnabulistic trance."

I returned to the office with Ilse, lifting her arm to demonstrate catalepsy. Then I said, "Ilse, go over there next to the man. I want you to stand like that until you put him into a trance. I'll come back in fifteen minutes."

He had already directed resistance toward me. How can you resist an already hypnotized person, who proceeds to hypnotize you?

And when I returned, he was in a deep trance.

You walk around resistance. You evoke all the resistance you can in *that* chair and have her sit in *this* chair. She leaves her resistance *there* and she has none when she reaches *this* chair.

When Erickson talks about "directing resistance," he is apply-ing the same principle he uses when he "directs" or "places" a symptom into a particular geographical position. For example, he will have a patient experience all the power of his airplane phobia in one chair. He will then direct the patient to "really experience the phobia in that chair" and then to "leave it in that chair." The implication is that he will not experience it anywhere else— only in that chair.

The doctor in this story had directed his resistance to hypnosis toward Erickson. Therefore he was not resistant toward others— certainly not toward a person who was obviously in a cataleptic trance herself.

CACTI

Usually I send alcoholic patients to AA because AA can do a better job than I can do. An alcoholic came to me and he said, "My grandparents on both sides were alcoholics; my parents were alcoholics; my wife's parents were alcoholics; my wife is an alco-holic and I have had delirium tremors eleven times. I am sick of being an alcoholic. My brother is an alcoholic too. Now, that is a hell of a job for you. What do you think you can do about it?"

I asked him what his occupation was.

"When I am sober I work on a newspaper. And alcohol is an occupational hazard there."

I said, "All right, you want me to do something about it—with that history. Now, the thing I am going to suggest to you won't seem the right thing. You go out to the Botanical Gardens. You look at all the cacti there and marvel at cacti that can survive three years without water, without rain. And do a lot of thinking."

Many years later a young woman came in and said, "Dr. Erickson, you knew me when I was three years old. I moved to California when I was three years old. Now I am in Phoenix and I came to see what kind of a man you were—what you looked like."

I said, "Take a good look, and I'm curious to know why you want to look at me."

She said, "Any man who would send an alcoholic out to the Botanical Gardens to look around, to learn how to get around without alcohol, and have it work, is the kind of man I want to see! My mother and father have been sober ever since you sent my father out there."

"What is your father doing now?"

"He's working for a magazine. He got out of the newspaper business. He says the newspaper business has an occupational hazard of alcoholism."

Now, that was a nice way to cure an alcoholic. Get him to respect cacti that survive three years without rain. You see you can talk about your textbooks. Today you take up this much. Tomorrow you take up that much. They say you do such and such. But actually you ought to look at your patient to figure out what kind of a man he is—or woman—then deal with the patient in a way that fits his or her problem, his or her unique problem.

This story is a beautiful example of indirect suggestion, applied symbolically.

COMPETITION

I had a patient come in from Philadelphia. A doctor brought him. I looked at that patient and I know that never before had I seen a man who was so competitive in nature. He would compete with you on anything and he had a very competitive business. He watched for every possible chance to compete.

I told him, "You have headaches, migraine headaches, that simply are killing you day after day. You've had them for nine years. You've been in daily treatment for your headaches for three years, with this doctor whom you trust. And you have made no progress at all. Now he has brought you out here, for me to work with you. And I'm *not* going to work with you, but I will do this. You put your hands on your knees and see whether your left hand will rise up to your face first or your right hand first."

And the competition that developed between his two hands —it was marvelous! It took about a half an hour for one hand to win.

Just when his hand was touching his face, I said, "The tension is in the muscles and you hold that tension in your hands while they are competing." It wasn't pleasant for him to feel that tension. "Now, if you want to have headaches, why not have a headache free of muscle competition of the muscles in your neck and shoulders? I don't think you want a headache any more than you want competition in your neck and shoulder muscles. I'd like to have you know what muscle relaxation is by letting your hands compete in relaxing."

So I gave him a lesson in tension and relaxation. And he's been free of headaches ever since. That was at least six or eight years ago.

Here Erickson illustrates the principle of meeting the patient in the patient's own frame of reference. He utilized the patient's competitive tendency and finally helped transfer this competitiveness into a more constructive direction. Of course, any competitiveness with Erickson was redirected toward the patient's inner competitiveness. Subsequently there was no resistance toward hypnosis or to the therapeutic suggestions that Erickson presented.

WET DREAMS

A woman had secured a divorce because she went all numb sexually and this had troubled her husband very much. He couldn't stand living with an unresponsive woman.

Then she had a number of boyfriends. She was now living with a man who was separated from his wife—a terribly sordid life. He wanted to have her as his mistress. He placed his children first, his wife second, his mistress third. And she didn't have any response at all.

The man was a wealthy man. He gave the woman a lot of things she liked. And she said, "I'm just plain cold. I have no feelings. It's a mechanical thing for me."

In a trance, I explained to her about how boys learn to recognize different feelings in their penis—when it's limp, a quarter erect, halfway erect, fully erect. How it feels when detumescence occurs. How it feels when the ejaculation occurs. And I explained to her all about wet dreams in boys.

I said, "In every boy half of his ancestors are feminine. And what any boy can do, any girl can do. And so *you* can have a wet dream at night. In fact, you can have a wet dream any time you wish. In the daytime you may see a handsome man. Why not have one then? He doesn't need to know about it. But *you* can know about it."

She said, "That's an intriguing thought."

I noticed that she became abnormally still. Her face flushed.

She said, "Dr. Erickson, you've just given me my first orgasm. Thank you very much."

I've received several letters from her. She's gotten rid of the boyfriend who separated from his wife. She's with a young man her age who's interested in marriage. And sex with him is absolutely wonderful. She has an orgasm or two or three every time.

Regarding that buildup about all boys having wet dreams, the reason for it is that a person learns to masturbate using his hands. In order to mature he must function sexually without the use of his hands. So his unconscious mind furnishes him, in his dreams, with a sex object.

Why did I describe boys' masturbation and not girls'? Because I could describe a boy and not be talking about her, and she could understand. And then, when she understood, I said, "A girl can have wet dreams too. And half of every boy's ancestors are female."

Erickson points out, apparently irrelevantly, "In every boy, half of his ancestors are feminine." He is simply telling this patient that she can learn from the experience that he has described for a boy.

We note not only that the patient's sexual unresponsiveness has been cured, but also that there was a carryover effect into her life, as manifested by her choosing a more appropriate partner. So much for the minimizing of hypnosis as "just symptom cure!"

This story is another good example of the use of indirect suggestion to bring about symptom cure.

PRETEND A TRANCE

Putting Dolly into a trance was quite a bit of labor. She just couldn't go deeply into a trance. I gave her a suggestion to the effect that she could "learn to go into a trance."

Then I told her about the experience of a hypnotic subject in

Albuquerque. A professor had been working with her, on some hypnotic experimentation, and he had told me, "We tried and tried to have her go into a deep trance and she simply can't."

So I had the subject essentially make believe she was going into a trance. I told her to open her eyes and just *be able to see my hand.* Then I told her that her peripheral vision would close down and down, until it was limited to my hand. And there are four other sensory areas. And pretty soon she felt sure that she could *see only my hand,* without the desk, or me, or the chair. Then I had her come out and go into her light trance, then repeat going into *a deep trance.* She repeatedly simulated a deep trance until it actually became real.

Dolly listened to that story. She simulated a deep trance— until it became real.

On occasion, members of an audience who heard Erickson tell this tale would, themselves, go into a deep trance. I have indicated some of the "marked" phrases. Here, Erickson changed his tone of voice and slowed down. These phrases were then responded to as if they were direct suggestions—such as "You will see only my hand."

With patients who have difficulty in going into a trance, I often quote recent research that indicates that people who simu-late a hypnotic trance will achieve the same results as those who are "actually" in a trance. As we can see in this tale, one can simulate a light trance or a deep one. Erickson gives guidance by describing some of the phenomena of a deep trance—such as "negative hallucinations" (not being able to see the desk, the rest of his body, or the chair).

DO YOU HEAR IT?

A woman volunteered at a workshop to be a subject. She said that many people had worked with her for hours, but the suggestions had no effect.

So I quizzed her a little bit about herself. She was French. She named her favorite French food, told me about a French restaurant in New Orleans that she liked, and told me how much she enjoyed music. She described the music.

When she saw my listening attitude, she turned her head and started listening with the other ear. She was left-eared. So I closed my right ear.

I said, "Do you hear it too? Is it very faint? I wonder how far away that orchestra is. It seems to be coming closer."

And pretty soon she found herself unable to keep from beating time to the music.

Then I raised the question, "Are there one or two violinists in the orchestra?" There were two. She pointed out the man who played the saxophone. And, so, we had a good time.

I wondered if the orchestra had reached the end of that piece of music and whether they opened their music notes for another type of music to play. She heard all her favorite tunes played.

Hypnosis is best accomplished by thinking about certain phenomena. You listen to a stutterer talk, and you can't resist forming the words yourself. You form the words yourself, to help him out.

This is a much more elegant way of suggesting auditory hallucinations than the usual one, in which the hypnotist will say, "You will hear . . ." Erickson is pointing out, again, the human tendency to want to help another person. Thus, when he shows himself almost able to hear the orchestra, his patient helps him by hearing it herself.

SKIN CONDITIONS

A woman doctor from the East called me up and said, "My son's a student at Harvard and he has an extremely bad case of acne. Can you treat that with hypnosis?"

I said, "Yes. Why bother bringing him to me? How are you going to spend Christmas vacation?"

She said, "I usually take a vacation from medical practice and go to Sun Valley and ski."

I said, "Well, this Christmas vacation, why don't you take your son with you? Find a cabin and remove all mirrors in it. You can eat your meals in that cabin, and be sure that you keep your hand mirror in the safety pocket of your purse."

They spent the time skiing and the son couldn't see a mirror. His acne cleared up in two weeks' time.

Now, acne can be cured by removing all mirrors. Rashes on the face or eczema often disappear in the same way.

Another patient, a woman with warts on both hands, deforming warts, came to see me. Her face was also a mess of warts. She said she wanted to get rid of them by hypnosis. If you know anything about medicine, you know that warts are caused by a virus and also that warts are very susceptible to changes in blood pressure.

I told the woman to soak her feet, first in ice-cold water, then in water as hot as she could stand, and then in ice-cold water again. She was to do that three times a day, until she was so annoyed that she'd give anything not to have to do it. When she had lost her warts she could *forget* about soaking her feet.

Now, it would be an annoying thing for her to have to interrupt the day's procedures to soak her feet and to keep this up in a scheduled manner.

Some three years later, this woman brought her son to me. I asked her about her warts. She said, "What warts?"

I said, "You came to see me, about three years ago, for the treatment of warts on your hands and face."

She said, "You must be mistaking me for another person." She had obeyed my suggestion. She had soaked her feet some months, as her husband confirmed. Then she got so disgusted by it, she forgot about soaking her feet, thereby forgetting about her warts. Since she was no longer worrying about her warts, their blood supply was cut down by the blood drawn to her feet and by her lack of attention to them. So she lost them all.

In the treatment of skin conditions by changing a person's focus of attention, Erickson is illustrating the dictum that Paracelsus expounded in the fifteenth century: "As man imagines himself to be, so shall he be, and he is that which he imagines." There really are physical effects associated with mental imagery. These effects can be attained inside of the body also, but they simply are more demonstrable on the skin. The most obvious examples are blushing when we think about an embarrassing situation, or the development of an erection when we fantasize an erotic image. A person who imagines himself as worthy holds himself erect and moves decisively and confidently. Is it, then, surprising that his skeletal structure, muscle tone, and facial expression develop quite differently from those of someone who "imagines" or images himself to be a nonentity?

"AUTO"—HYPNOSIS

One patient said to me, "I'm very neurotic, but I can't talk to you or anybody else. I know you through some friends of mine who are your patients. And I haven't got the nerve to tell you what my problem is. Now will you be my therapist?"

I said, "Yes, in any way I can."

She said, "Well, the way I'm going to do it is this. In the evening, around eleven o'clock, I'll drive over and park in your driveway and imagine you're in the car with me. Then I'll think through my problem."

She paid for two consultations. I don't know how many times she spent the night, until about 4 A.M., in my driveway working on her problem. She worked out her problem and only paid me for the first two consultations.

She told me, "I'm over my problem. Now if you want me to, I'll work on experimental work with you." And Linn Cooper [co-author with Erickson of *Time Distortion in Hypnosis*] and I used her in time-distortion experiments with hypnosis. So, in actuality, she really paid, in time services. And I suggested she use the trance, when Linn Cooper and I worked on time distortion, to her own advantage. Linn Cooper and I were satisfied. We were getting what we wanted. I think she got all she wanted.

In this case we have a literal example of Erickson's dictum "It's the patient who does the therapy." Still, this patient needed to know that Erickson was her therapist. She obviously could not treat herself without a therapist. Perhaps this need for another person, a therapist—if only in fantasy—confirms Martin Buber's teaching that only in relationship with other people can we be fulfilled and enabled to grow.

DELVING

When my daughter was in medical school she read a paper on double binds by Ernest Rossi and me. She came in and said, "So that's how I do it!"

Rossi asked her, "That's how you do what?"

She said, "All patients have the right to refuse a rectal, hernial, or vaginal examination by a medical student. None of the other female students have done any and I have done vaginal, rectal, and hernial examinations on every one of my patients."

I asked her how she did it, since they all had the right to refuse.

She said, "When I got to that part of the examination I smiled prettily and said very sympathetically, 'I know you are tired of me peering into your eyes and peeking into your ears and up your nose and down your throat, poking you here and thumping you there. Now, as soon as I do the rectal and hernial you can say good-bye to me.'"

And they all waited patiently to say good-bye to her.

This approach is an excellent example of the setting up of a double bind. In order for the weary patients to get Kristi to leave them alone, they must first permit her to do the rectal, vaginal, and hernial exams. First, though, she joined them by verbalizing their weariness and their desire to be left alone.

When this tale was told to me, it evoked, by indirect suggestion, the feeling that I should ask Erickson, "Go ahead. Do the rectal." In other words, I felt that he was asking for permission to delve deeper into my unconscious mind. I immediately found myself remembering long-forgotten early childhood memories of enemas. I have found that when patients feel that they are being helped, or even forced to bring out deeply buried "gut feelings" and memories, they will often dream or fantasize about enemas or rectal examinations. The focusing on vaginal and hernial examinations might very well, in some patients, bring forth associations to sexual feelings and experiences.

KATHLEEN: TREATMENT OF A PHOBIA

In the following complete transcript, we can, fortunately, observe an entire therapy demonstrating indirect suggestion. We can see the ways in which Erickson seeds ideas and comes back to them later. We can observe his utilization of long-term post-hypnotic suggestion and reframing.

The subject of this verbatim account, Kathleen, was a student in one of Erickson's teaching seminars. It is not possible for us to determine how Erickson discovered that she was suffering with a vomiting phobia. He simply explains, when asked, that "In this world there are always a number of tattletales." Perhaps another student had told him. Or perhaps he deduced it. In any case, he was not hesitant in proffering treatment, and it was accepted.

E: You realize you're in a trance, don't you? You can realize it better if you close your eyes.

Now, in that trance, I want you to feel so comfortable. I want you to go into trance so deeply that it will seem to you as if you are a bodyless mind, that your mind is floating in space, free of your body, floating in space and floating in time.

And I want you to choose some time in the past when you were a very, very little girl. And my voice will go with you. And my voice will change into that of your parents, your neighbors, your friends, your schoolmates, your playmates, your teachers. And I want you to find yourself sitting in the schoolroom, a little girl feeling very happy about something, something that happened a long time ago, that you forgot a long time ago.

And there's one other experience I want you to have. And when I tell you to wake up, to wake up from the neck up. Your body will remain sound asleep. Now, it will be hard to awaken from the neck up, but you can do it.

Now, soon you'll begin awakening from the neck up. Now, don't be scared, because your body is sound asleep. Take all the time necessary to wake up from the neck up. It's hard work, but you can do it.

(long pause)

Now your head is beginning to wake up. Your eyes are beginning to open. (pause) You can do it. And maybe your body, still sound asleep, will be that of a little girl. You are slowly awakening from the neck up. Your eyes are beginning to flutter open. As you lift your head, your neck unfreezes. (pause)

Lift the head and see me.

Is your head awake?

You know that in this world, there are many adaptations to life. I would hate to go for a swim in the Arctic Ocean, but the walrus enjoys it; the whale enjoys it. I think the Antarctic is cold. I'd hate to be a penguin hatching an egg at sixty below zero, holding that egg between my feet, and starving for six weeks until my fat spouse came back from the ocean and took her turn hatching the egg.

And, you know, the whales, such large mammals, live on plankton, microscopic particles in the ocean water. And I wonder how many tons of sea water pass through the mouth before they get enough plankton. Because, you know, I'm glad the whale can eat plankton and grow large and fat. And the famous scuba divers of Australia enjoy riding on the back of the leopard shark as it swims lazily about, passing seawater over its gills for oxygen, and combing its gills for plankton to nourish its huge body.

Do you have any objection to whales and sharks living that way? And then I watched an education program of a woodpecker in the Black Forest, made by a bird-watcher. The woodpecker spent about three weeks chipping out a hole big enough and deep enough to rear a family in. The bird-watcher, in the absence of the parents on feeding trips, bored a hole in the nest and pushed away the wood, and put a pane of glass into place so the woodpecker's hole was a complete hole, solid and impenetrable. Then the bird-watcher fixed up an electric light so when the eggs hatched, their rate of growth could be filmed. Finally, he fitted a ring around the neck of the young woodpecker, and during the absence of the parent, he emptied out the throat of the baby woodpecker to see what kind of food it was living on. In that way he discovered that the woodpecker is vital to the preservation of the forest. He found leaf-eating beetles and wood-eating beetles that destroy the bark and leaves of the tree.

Of course, the parents go out to locate the beetles; they have puffs in their necks in which they predigest those hard beetles. And when they get back to the nest, they regurgitate the half-digested beetles into the gaping mouths of the nestlings.

I think nursing, from my experience, is a much better way of getting food. If I were a woodpecker's baby, I'd much prefer the regurgitated beetles, already predigested. And so, human beings are the highest of all animals in development, but all these learnings so peculiar to other animals yet have their counterparts in human life. We use regurgitation to save life. Woodpeckers use regurgitation to save life. Human beings swallow things instantly only to have their stomach say, "You pitiful fool, get rid of this, now, and by the shortest route possible." Isn't that right?

And I think it's wonderful that human beings have stomachs without brains and yet have enough intelligence to say, "Get rid of this rubbish, in the quickest route possible."

Now, all these things in human living are very, very important and should be admired.

Now, do you think you're ever going to be afraid of vomiting again? No need to be. It's nice you don't have to depend on brains in your head. And you could say the reaction is often much more intelligent than mental reactions.

So, would you like to tell us how you used to be afraid of vomiting?

Kathleen: How did you know that?

E: In this world there are always a number of tattletales. Do you know when you developed your vomiting phobia?

K: A long time ago.

E: Do you know the phrase "ontogeny repeats philogeny"? The growth of the individual repeats the growth of the species. Though you might breathe through your nose, anatomically there are gill slits. How does it feel to be wide awake? How large is your body? Doesn't it amaze you that you can't use it? No, you can't stand up.

K: What can't I do?"

E: You can't stand up.

K: Are you sure?

E: Oh, I'm sure, but are you?

K: Well, I was till a minute ago; I think I can.

E: Practically everybody here *knows* they can. You only think you can.

K: Well, I know I could until a minute ago. I've always had a great fear of not being able to move, or being crippled like my mother.

E: What crippled her?

K: For years I thought it was polio, but then I found out it was her mind. She had polio, but it was her mind.

E: Mine is really polio, plus wear and tear of age. Someday, like the one-hoss shay, I'm going to fall apart. I intend to stick around until that day, though.

You know, when I was a little child I visited my grandmother's brother and his family. They were shearing sheep. I heard the sheep bleating. I ran away because I couldn't understand shearing the sheep. My Aunt Mary served fried liver, and for years I wouldn't eat liver because I thought of those sheep's ears. Now, with my gout, I can't eat all the liver I'd like to.

Close your eyes, and wake up all over now. All over.

Wake up all over. And free. And try to keep the smile off your face.

Now, what do you think about vomiting?

It's like when you have too many cans of soda pop; when you've gotta go, you've gotta go.

K: Do you have a secret stable of tattletales?

E: Your friend came in this morning and said you had a bad dream, remembering only the affects. That told me you have a phobia. One of my tattletales named the phobia. Aren't you glad there are tattletales? Do you believe in reincarnation?

K: I'm going to come back as a French horn.

E: I think you have to tip it over and drain it.

K: You know, all my life I've been coming back as a French horn without knowing that! I get the picture now; all I had was the sound before!

E: Let this be a lesson to you: all your brains are not located in your cranium. You know what Shakespeare says: "The stages of life really start with the infant."

Now *I* think you ought to have a *good* start in life.

And in Corinthians it says: "When I was a child, I spoke as a child. I did as a child. And now I have become a man I put aside childish things." And that includes fears, right?

What is your first name?"

K: Kathy.

E: Shall I officially change it for you? From now on, it shall be only Kathleen, not fraidy-cat, puking Kathy.

How do you feel?

K: Somewhere between spacey and peaceful.

E: There's an old Irish song; I don't want to call my wife out to quote it. I never quote exactly correctly. I wanted to introduce Margaret Mead saying I couldn't quote poetry correctly. But I have no difficulty introducing Dr. Margaret Mead. And the one other thing I was sure of: I could quote Gertrude Epstein's "A Rose is a Rose is a Rose is a Rose." Only to find out later from my family, who enjoyed it, that Gertrude Stein's name didn't have an "Ep," and that there are only three roses!

Now, the thing I have in mind is "Down went McGinty to the bottom of the sea." If the sea was Irish whiskey, he swore he'd never come up again. If the sea was dry, he wouldn't waste one drop of the sea by vomiting it!

And Kathleen is a good Irish name!

Now you have witnessed a demonstration of psychotherapy. I was not the least bit dignified. I laughed and I joked. I may have bored the life out of some of you by talking about whales and plankton and so on. Woodpeckers and beetles.

The above transcript is so rich in examples of indirect suggestion and use of symbolic language that it would take an entire book to discuss these aspects. Readers may enjoy discovering some of them for themselves.

By a roundabout route, starting with all types of different animals and their adaptation, Erickson introduces the idea that vomiting is a lifesaving adaptive reaction in human beings. He talks about the "gut reaction" as being valuable. He introduces his optimistic philosophy of life to counter the patient's fear of becoming crippled, "like my mother." He says, "Someday, like the one-hoss shay, I am going to fall apart. I intend to stick around until that day, though." He drives home and validates her cure by reference to the "infant" of Shakespeare, and he leaves out the end of the quotation so that the patient herself can supply it. ("First the infant, mewling and puking in his mother's arms.") To make sure she gets the message, he refers to the passage from Corinthians that says, ". . . and now that I have become a man, I have put aside childish things." He adds, "And that includes fears, right?" To change her attitudes toward herself, he even changes her name to Kathleen, so that she can leave behind her previous attitude toward herself, which includes her being "a fraidy-cat, puking Kathy." He concludes with "Now you have witnessed a demonstration in psychotherapy." And an elegant demonstration it was!

Erickson utilizes every production or comment of the patient toward his therapeutic goal—in this case, to change her attitude about vomiting. For example, when she says that she would like to be reincarnated as a French horn, he immediately responds by saying, "I think you have to tip it over and drain it." In other words, she has to be prepared to empty out whatever fluids have accumulated in her. She has to be ready to vomit. Kathleen signifies her recognition of this suggestion by saying, "All I had was the sound before." She is saying that there is some substance that can be brought up from inside her.

When Erickson utilizes quotations from Shakespeare and the Bible, he is relating to his patient as if she were a young student, open to learning. He seeded this idea in the initial hypnotic suggestion when he said, "And I want you to find yourself sitting in the schoolroom." In this case, Erickson takes a rather scatter-shot approach. He can't be certain which set of suggestions or which way of reframing the problem would be utilized by the patient, so he seems to hit her from all sides.

There is no escaping his suggestions of health. He even lifts her out of her mess, when he gives her a new name, a new identity. Her new name will be associated in an almost Pavlovian way with the change. Erickson used this approach, giving people new names or allowing them to give themselves new names, long before this practice became popular in the encounter groups of the sixties. The new name becomes a posthypnotic cue so that every time she uses it or hears it, new associations of mastery or self-respect will be revivified. This approach is much more aesthetically pleasing, naturalistic, and geared to the individual than is, for example, biofeedback treatment, wherein cues are mechanistically introduced. For example, in one treatment of hypertension by means of biofeedback, patients were conditioned to have their blood pressure lowered every time they looked at a red dot on their watches. Erickson's cue—in this case the name Kathleen—is beautifully woven in with all of the other cues and suggestions. *Jeffrey Zeig's comment was "He gave this woman a forced feeding. He gave her an ingestion of new material that she would have to incorporate, and that she could not regurgitate." And wasn't it aesthetically and tastefully presented?*

5. Overcoming Habitual Limitations

In the following stories, Erickson explains two elements that are very important in extending limits. The first is establishing a mental set that is broader or less limited than the preceding one. The second is to approach the task without focusing on the limits, but focusing on the task itself. In golf, for example, "On every hole you think it is the first." In other words, the sense of an entire context, including the number of the hole, the previous scores, and so on, is eliminated while one focuses on each stroke, each shot. The question of limits, then, does not arise. That is determined later when one looks back at the score.

If you want to become creative or to think creatively, you must practice what has been called "divergent thinking," in contrast to "convergent thinking," which adults tend to adopt as they become more and more restrictive in their behavior. In convergent thinking, a number of stories or a number of themes converge into one. In divergent thinking, one idea moves out into many different directions, like the branching of a tree. A book that I have found helpful in stimulating imagination and, perhaps, increasing creativity is Mental Jogging, by Reid J. Daitzman. It includes 365 mental exercises along the lines of "Name seven ways to avoid spilling coffee while driving."

These tales are typical of those that Erickson used to stretch people's minds.

STONES AND QUANTUM MECHANICS

All of you have seen my stones that were polished two hundred million years ago. My fifteen-year-old grandson said, "These stones were polished two hundred million years ago. That eliminates man. I ought to know how they were polished. You wouldn't show me a water-polished stone. I've lived in Okinawa; I've seen water-polished stones. And I've been around volcanos; it wouldn't be that. You're showing me something unexpected, from two hundred million years ago. I know you're showing me something that I know about. I've got to stop thinking about sand and water and ice, and man."

While he was cogitating about that I said, "I have another riddle to ask you. What does this refer to? 'How I want a drink, alcoholic of course, after the heavy chapters involving quantum mechanics.' "

He said, "I don't get it. I don't know what quantum mechanics are."

I said, "You don't need to know. I'll give you the illiterate answer. Drive two fenceposts into the ground two feet apart. Lay across the fenceposts a board just long enough to overlap the posts by an inch, and you get the illiterate answer."

It took Erickson's grandson a few minutes before he was able to exclaim, "That's the first time I've ever thought of it that way!" It may take most readers even longer to visualize the "illiterate" answer or to draw two vertical lines with a horizontal line above them—π— the symbol for "pi." Erickson gives another hint, one that would probably be helpful only for medical students and doctors of medicine. He says, "All doctors know the mnemonic for the cranial nerves, 'On old Olympus' towering tops a Finn and German vend some hops.' " Thus, instead of simply saying, "The riddle is a mnemonic," Erickson gives an example of another mnemonic, leaving it for the reader to make his own connections.

The stones that Erickson had shown his grandson came from the gizzard of a dinosaur. They were polished as the dinosaur digested his food. Thus, the grandson was correct in realizing that he had to think about something other than sand, water, ice, or man as the source of the polishing. He had to go outside his usual ways of thinking in order to solve that problem. Erickson is telling his readers and listeners that they must go outside of their usual ways of thinking. The riddle about the stones is not related to the other one, except that they are both riddles.

If the reader has not yet made the connection, he might try counting the number of letters in each word of "How I want a drink . . ." That's right! Pi is 3.14159265358979 . . .

GOING FROM ROOM TO ROOM

I asked a student, "How do you get from this room into that room?"

He answered, "First you stand up. Then you take a step . . ."

I stopped him and said, "Name all the possible ways you can get from this room into that room."

He said, "You can go by running, by walking; you can go by jumping; you can go by hopping; by somersaulting. You can go out that door, go outside the house, come in another door and into the room. Or you could climb out a window if you want to . . ."

I said, "You said you would be inclusive but you made an omission, which is a major omission. I usually illustrate, first, by saying, 'If I want to get into that room from this room, I would go out that door, take a taxi to the airport, buy a ticket to Chicago,

New York, London, Rome, Athens, Hong Kong, Honolulu, San Francisco, Chicago, Dallas, Phoenix, come back by limousine and go in the back yard and then through the back gate into the back door and into that room.' And you thought only of forward movement! You didn't think of going in backwards, did you? And you didn't think of crawling in."

The student added, "Or of sliding on my stomach either."

We do limit ourselves so terribly in all of our thinking!

I WIN OLYMPIC CHAMPIONSHIPS
ALL THE TIME

I asked Erickson about a patient of mine who is a concert pianist. He was fearful that he would freeze at the keyboard and that he would be unable to play because of arthritis in his hands. Erickson's response was as follows:

A pianist, no matter how bad his hands get, knows music. And he knows how to compose. And that's one thing he should never forget. A hand may get useless, but he can compose, and compose even better. Out of a wheelchair *I win Olympic championships all the time.*

DONALD LAWRENCE AND THE
GOLD MEDAL

Donald Lawrence had been practicing the shot put for a whole year. The coach at the high school had voluntarily coached him, without charge, for a whole year, every night. Donald was six feet six inches, 260 pounds, and didn't have an ounce of fat on him, and the coach had a great ambition to get a national high-school record for the shot put. At the end of the year the high-school contest was two weeks away and Donald could only put the shot fifty-eight feet—far short of the record.

His father was interested. He brought Donald in to see me. I told Donald to sit down and go into a trance. I told him to levitate his hand and to learn to feel his muscles all over and then to come in the next time, go into a trance, and listen to me. I asked him if he knew that a mile used to be four minutes long and that Roger Bannister had broken the record—after the record had stood for many, many years. I asked him if he knew *how* Bannister had done this.

I said, "Well, Bannister, who was acquainted with sports of all kinds, realized that you can win a ski run by a hundredth of a second, by a tenth of a second; and then he began to realize that a four-minute mile would be 240 seconds. If he could run it in 239 and five-tenths of a second he would break the four-minute mile. Having thought that through, he broke the four-minute-mile record."

And I said, "You have already thrown the shot fifty-eight feet. And, Donald, tell me honestly, do you think you know the difference between fifty-eight feet and fifty-eight feet and one-sixteenth of an inch?"

He said, "No, of course not."

I said, "Fifty-eight feet and fifty-eight feet and one-eighth of an inch?"

He said, "No."

And I brought it up to fifty-eight feet and fifty-nine feet and he could not tell the difference. I had a couple more sessions in which *I slowly enlarged the possibility.* And two weeks later he set a national high-school record.

That summer he came in and said, "I am going to the Olympics; I want some advice."

I said, "The Olympic record for the shot put is just under sixty-two feet. You are just an eighteen-year-old kid. It would be all right if you bring home the bronze medal. And don't bring home the silver or the gold. Because then you will be competing against yourself. Let Perry and O'Bryan take the gold and silver."

Perry and O'Bryan did. And Donald came home with a bronze medal.

Then the Olympics were in Mexico City. Donald came in and said, "I am going to Mexico City."

I said, "You are four years older now, Donald. It would be all right if you take the gold medal." And he came home with the gold medal.

He was going to Tokyo and asked, "What shall I do in Tokyo?"

I said, "Athletic accomplishments require time for maturing. Take the gold medal again."

He came home with it, and he entered college to study dentistry. There he found out that he was eligible for two meets that he wanted to enter. He came in and said, "The college meet is coming up; it's official. What shall I do about the shot put?"

I said, "Donald, people always restrict themselves. In the shot put in the Olympics they restricted themselves for years and years to less than sixty-two feet. Frankly, I don't know how far a shot can be put. I am certain it can be put sixty-two feet. I even wonder if it can be put seventy feet. So why don't you reach a record mark, somewhere between sixty-two feet and seventy feet?" I think he placed it sixty-five feet, six inches.

The next time he came in and asked, "Now what do I do?"

I said, "Donald, you showed that the longtime Olympic record was very wrong, by getting it up to sixty-five feet. And that's just the first *try*. Next time see how close you can get it to seventy feet."

Donald said, "All right."

He placed it sixty-eight feet, ten inches.

I told the coach at Texas A & M all about Donald Lawrence, how I trained him. The coach listened very carefully and said, "I am training Masterson for the shot put."

When the coach told Masterson how I had trained Donald Lawrence, Masterson said, "If that's the way Erickson trained Donald Lawrence to set a record, I am going to see how much farther I can put it than Donald Lawrence."

He placed it seventy feet. I think it is up to seventy feet and four inches now.

Erickson then switches to golf:

In golf, actually, you hit the first hole and reach the second hole in a correct number of shots. Then the question arises, "Can you do as well on the third hole?" Therefore, on every hole you *think* it's the first. You let the caddy keep count of which hole.

One contestant came to me and said, "I shoot in the low seventies and I want to win the state championship before I go into professional golfing. I want to win the amateur championship of Arizona. But every tournament I enter, I wind up with a score in the nineties. Playing alone I can get down to the low seventies."

I put him into a trance and told him, "You will play only the *first* hole. That's all you will remember. And you will be *alone* on the golf course."

He played in the next state tournament. After the eighteenth hole he walked toward another hole, and somebody stopped him and told him, "You have played the eighteenth hole." And he said, "No, I just played the first hole." Then he said, "Where did all these people come from?"

We can note the way Erickson uses truisms to give suggestions. "You're four years older now, Donald. It would be all right if you take the gold medal." The first statement is true; the second part of the statement could be true. By juxtaposing them, Erickson equates one with the other. By suggesting to Donald that he first bring home the bronze medal, he is demonstrating an inordi-

nate amount of control—a pinpoint control. This kind of control is even better than winning first place. When, four years later, Erickson suggests that it is all right for Donald to get the gold medal, this had been predicated on previous demonstrations of control. Finally, it is important with this story, more than with some of the others, to remember that Donald Lawrence is a real person and that he actually has won Olympic championships. Only his name is disguised, along with minor facts. This kind of beneficial effect was neither purely theoretical nor was it a fantasy of Erickson's. Donald was able to make his progress step by step. Erickson started by reminding him of something he already knew: Roger Bannister had broken the record for the four-minute mile. How did Bannister do this? By changing his way of thinking. He changed the four minutes to 240 seconds, and then he could deal with seconds instead of minutes. Erickson's strategy was then to get Donald to think about things in a different way. Once he changed his thinking, like Roger Bannister, he was able to overcome the psychological block. Erickson also makes a small change —the difference between fifty-eight feet and fifty-eight feet and one-sixteenth of an inch. He makes a small change, and then he builds upon that change.

Each problem carries a past and a future. What Erickson realizes is that if you eliminate the past and change the future, you've changed two-thirds of the problem. Therefore, if you think about each hole as being the first, there is no anxiety from the past. You have eliminated the past and you can change the future because the future can only be one of positive expectancy.

These two tales have been very helpful to me when I convey the idea to patients that the answer to dependence upon another person is to extend one's own capabilities and limits. This is much more meaningful than simply telling them that they must learn to stand on their own two feet, which is what everybody else has been telling them.

TRAINING THE U.S. RIFLE TEAM
TO BEAT THE RUSSIANS

The coach of the advanced marksmanship team of the army got to reading about hypnosis and decided that hypnosis could help his team beat the Russians. The teams were training in Georgia. They had been in a shoot in San Francisco and they stopped in Phoenix. The coach brought the team in to see me and asked me if I could train his team to beat the Russians in the international shoot.

I explained to him, "I've shot a rifle twice, when I was a teenager. I know the muzzle end and the stock end—that's all I know about a rifle. Now, these riflemen know all they need to know about a gun. I'm a medical man. I know what I need to know about a body. I'll train your team. They already have the rifle knowledge and I have the medical knowledge."

The commandant was so infuriated that a civilian was going to train the rifle team that he added two men who had been trying for two years to make the rifle team. I don't know what the qualifications were for the rifle team, but it was a score in the sixties. Those two men had been devoting all their spare time to training and scored in the low forties. In other words, they couldn't make the team.

One of the first things I told the man, after I found that in the contest you shoot forty rounds in succession, was, "I know the first bulls-eye is easy. The question is 'Can you do it twice? . . . Can you do it eleven times, after ten successive bulls-eyes? . . . You've done it nineteen times. Will you make it the *twentieth* time? . . . The tension is growing—with each successful shot!

" 'You've made it twenty-nine times. *Can you make it thirty times?* . . . You've made it thirty-five times. Thirty-six? Thirty-seven? Thirty-eight? (breathlessly) Thirty-nine? Can I *possibly* make it *forty times?*' "

The next thing I did was to call in a good hypnotic subject. I told the subject, "After you awaken you're going to be offered a cigarette. You'll want to smoke it. And you'll gladly accept it. You'll put it into your mouth and you'll absentmindedly drop it . . . and take a second cigarette—not remembering you've had the first cigarette." And so—he accepted 169 cigarettes!

Then they knew that they too could forget. If *he* could forget 169 cigarettes, then *they* could forget each one of the forty shots.

Then I told them, "Now you fit the sole of your foot on the ground so that the sole of your foot feels comfortable. Then you make sure your ankle's comfortable, your calf is comfortable, your knee, your hip joint, your trunk, your left arm; your finger on the trigger; the rifle stock against your shoulder. Get just exactly the *right feeling*. And then you wave the rifle sight up and down, across the target and back and forth. And, at the right moment, you squeeze the trigger."

And they beat the Russians, for the first time, at Moscow. And the two men the commandant had thrown in *also* placed.

While the preceding tale illustrates the establishment of a broader or less limited mental set, this tale illustrates the principle of focusing on the task itself. This was accomplished, not only by the men's forgetting all preceding shots, but also by their focusing attention on sensations in the body, in the present.

A FLASH OF COLOR

A patient came to me and said, "I've lived in Phoenix for the past fifteen years and I have hated every moment of those fifteen years. My husband has offered me a vacation in Flagstaff. I hate Phoenix so much, but I have refused to go to Flagstaff. I prefer to stay in Phoenix and to *hate* being in Phoenix."

So I told her, while she was in a trance, that she would be curious about hating Phoenix and about why she punished herself so much. That should be a very *big* curiosity. "And there is another thing to be curious about—and very, very curious about. If you go to Flagstaff for a week, you will see, very unexpectedly, a flash of color." As long as she had a big curiosity about hating Phoenix, she could develop an *equally* large curiosity, just as compelling, to find out what that flash of color would be in Flagstaff.

She went to Flagstaff for a week, but stayed a month. What flash of color did she see? I had none in mind. I just wanted her to be curious. And when she saw that flash of color, she was so elated that she remained a whole month in Flagstaff. That flash of color was a redheaded woodpecker flying past an evergreen tree. This woman usually spends the summer in Flagstaff now, but she also has gone to the East Coast to see the color *there.* She has gone to Tucson, to see a flash of color. She has gone to New York, to see a flash of color. She has gone to Europe, to see a flash of color. And my statement that she would see a flash of color was based only upon the fact that you have to see a lot of things that ordinarily *you* don't see. And I wanted her to *keep looking.* And she would *find something* to translate into my words.

This set of instructions, which was included in a hypnotic induction, was used to help the listener overcome habitual limitations. The overt suggestions and permission for the overcoming of these limitations are obvious. I have italicized certain words, which Erickson "marked" by emphasizing them with a change of tone. These words, such as "keep looking," are obvious instructions presented in an embedded way to encourage looking into one's own unconscious repertory. Very often, after one of these words was marked, he paused, sometimes for as long as three or four minutes, to allow time for this inner work to take place. At the same time he includes posthypnotic suggestions, which would lead to a dream, perhaps a week later.

Bandler and Grinder might point out Erickson's switches of "representational systems" in this story. The patient begins kinesthetically by stating that she prefers to stay in Phoenix and to hate being in Phoenix. Erickson changes her representational system to a visual one, using, as a bridge, her curiosity. He dislodges her from her hate to curiosity, which decreases the hate. Then he moves the curiosity to something visual. In this way he goes stepwise from the kinesthetic to the visual.

Even though Erickson himelf could not appreciate color—he was color-blind—he used color just as he used sound and poetry (which he also could not appreciate, because he was tone deaf and lacked a sense of rhythm), because he knew that other people could appreciate these elements. Jeffrey Zeig has pointed out that by moving a patient beyond a limitation that he himself has, Erickson is encouraging the patient to "leave him in the dust." This is a nice way to emphasize individual differences. Also, if that particular patient is a "one-up" type of person, it gives him an opportunity to be even more "one-up."

He can have something that even Erickson can't.

WALKING ON GLARE ICE

During the war I worked at the induction board in Detroit. One day, as I was going to the induction board, I saw a veteran who had returned with an artificial leg, looking at some glare ice and eyeing it suspiciously because he knew that he was likely to fall on glare ice.

"That's very smooth ice," I told him. "Stand where you are. I'll come over and teach you how to walk on glare ice."

He could see that I had a limp, so he knew I must be talking about what I knew. He watched me walk across that glare ice and asked, "How did you do it?"

I said, "I won't tell you, I'll teach you. Now, you just keep your eyes totally shut." And I turned him around, and walked him back and forth on the ice-free sidewalk. I kept walking him back and forth over longer distances and then shorter and shorter distances until finally I noticed his utter confusion. Finally, I got him clear across to the other side of that glare ice.

I said, "Open your eyes."

He said, "Where is that glare ice?"

I said, "It's behind you."

He said, "How did I get over here?"

I said, "Now you can understand. You walked as if the cement was bare. When you try to walk on ice the usual tendency is to tense your muscles, preparing for a fall. You get a mental set. And you slip that way.

"If you put the weight of your legs down straight, the way you would on dry cement, you wouldn't slip. The slide comes because you don't put down your full weight and because you tense yourself."

It took me a long time to find that out. Did you ever walk upstairs one step too many? What an awful jolt it is! Walk downstairs one too many—you can break your leg. And yet you are totally unaware of that set.

Here, Erickson demonstrates his classical method of helping a person out of a fixed mental set. The first step is to confuse the subject. The second step, during this confused period, is to lead the subject over the obstacle so that the subject has an experience of success. Of course, in this case, the experience of success occurred when the subject failed to respond with his usual tightening, with his usual mental set. The old set is replaced with a new one. The patient believes he can walk across glare ice. He now approaches new "slippery" situations without carrying over the fear associated with previous "falls."

Sometimes, it is important for the patient to not use things he knows or perceptions that he ordinarily would use. For this reason, Erickson has the man close his eyes. Once the man had stopped seeing, he could accomplish the task. Seeing had previously caused him to have a kinesthetic reaction that caused him to adopt the wrong set.

Erickson liked to illustrate hypnotic concentration by asking people, "If I were to put a board one foot wide and fifty feet long on the floor, would you have any difficulty walking along it?" Of course, the answer would be "no." He would then add, "What would be your reaction if I were to put the same board—one foot wide and fifty feet long—between two buildings reaching across from the fiftieth floor of one to the fiftieth floor of the other?" Again, in this example, the visual sense is associated with a kinesthetic set that would lead most people to lose their sense of security. To succeed in this task, or in walking a tightrope, it may be important to not use something you have—that is, your visual sense (and your imagination).

THE TARAHUMARA INDIANS

The Tarahumara Indians of southwestern Chihuahua are the ones who can run a hundred miles—their pressure doesn't go up and their heartbeat doesn't change. Some entrepreneur took some hundred-mile runners to the Olympics (1928, Amsterdam). They didn't even place. Because, they thought twenty-five miles was when you warmed up! It hadn't been explained to them that their run was twenty-five miles long.

I sometimes think about that story when I am having difficulty getting into a task, when I am writing, repairing something around the house, frustrated by difficulties, or literally breathless from jogging. The phrase will come into my head—"I am just warming up now." I usually find more energy available after this.

DRY BEDS

As in Sufi tales or Zen stories, the recipient of the knowledge of the healer must be in a state of readiness to receive. In many of those stories the supplicant comes to the master but is refused entry until "the vehicle is ready to receive the riches of the teaching." Erickson often accomplishes this preparation by causing the listener or the patient to wait a long time before he delivers his "punch line." For example, when he presented the next tale to a group of students, he spent about one-half hour in building up to the final prescription. Some of this time was spent in outlining the background history. Some was spent in asking the listeners how they would treat such a patient. Some time was spent in telling other stories, not directly related to the problem. He repeated such phrases as "There is something that you know but don't know that you know. When you know what it is that you don't know you know, then you will be able to have a permanently dry bed." This type of puzzling and yet intriguing statement causes the listeners to do what Ernest Rossi has called an "inner search." The listener is thus already beginning to search inside himself for resources that may help in the healing process. When we consider one of Erickson's induction technique, the "waiting technique," the same principle applies. The patient literally is left begging for more. Then he is ready to receive.

A mother brought her eleven-year-old daughter in to see me. As soon as I heard about her bed-wetting, I sent the mother out of the room with the belief that the girl could tell me her story. The girl told me that she had a bladder infection in very early infancy, that she was treated by a urologist, and that the infection had persisted for five or six years, maybe longer. She had been cystoscoped regularly, hundreds of times, and eventually the focus of the infection was found in one kidney. That had been removed and she had been free of infections for about four years. She had been cystoscoped so many hundreds of times, and her bladder and sphincter were so stretched, that she wet the bed every night, as soon as her bladder relaxed in her sleep. During the day she could forcibly control her bladder, unless she laughed. The relaxation that goes with laughter caused her to wet her pants.

Her parents thought that since she had had her kidney removed and had been free of the infection for several years, she ought to learn to control herself. She had three younger sisters, who called her bad names and ridiculed her. All of the mothers knew that she wet her bed. And all the schoolchildren, two or three thousand of them, knew that she was a bed wetter and that she wet her pants when she laughed. So she was the butt of much ridicule.

She was very tall, very pretty, blond, with long hair that reached down to her waist. She was really a very charming girl. She was ostracized, ridiculed; more was demanded of her than she could produce. She had to endure the pity of neighbors and the ridicule of her sisters and the schoolchildren. She couldn't go to slumber parties or spend the night with relatives because of her bed-wetting. I asked her if she had seen any other doctors. She said that she had seen a lot of them, had swallowed a barrel full of pills and a barrel full of medicine, and nothing helped.

I told her that I was like all the other doctors. I couldn't help her either. "But you already know something but you don't know that you know it. As soon as you find out what it is that you already know and don't know that you know, you can begin having a dry bed."

Then I told her, "I am going to ask you a very simple question and I want a very simple answer. Now, here's the question. If you were sitting in the bathroom, urinating, and a strange man poked his head in the doorway, what would you do?"

"I'd freeze!"

"That's right. You'd freeze—and stop urinating. Now, you know what you already knew, but didn't know that you already knew it. Namely, that you can stop urinating at any time for any stimulus you choose. You really don't need a strange man poking his head in the bathroom. Just the *idea* of it is enough. You'll stop. You'll freeze. And when he goes away you will start urinating.

"Now, having a dry bed is a very difficult job. You might have your first dry bed in two weeks. And there has to be a lot of practice, starting and stopping. Some days you may forget to practice starting and stopping. That's all right. Your body will be good to you. It will always give you further opportunities. And some days you may be too busy to practice starting and stopping, but that's all right. Your body will always give you opportunities to start and stop. It would surprise me very much if you had a permanently dry bed within three months. It would also surprise me if you didn't have a permanently dry bed within six months. And the first dry bed will be much easier than two dry beds in succession. And three dry beds in succession is much harder. And four dry beds in succession is still harder. After that it gets easier. You can have five, six, seven, a whole week of dry beds. And then you can know that you can have one week of dry beds and another week of dry beds."

I took my time with the girl. I had nothing else to do. I spent an hour and a half with her and dismissed her. About two weeks later she brought in this present for me—the first present she had ever given with the knowledge that she had had a dry bed (it was a knitted purple cow). I value that present. And six months later she was staying overnight at friends', relatives', at slumber parties, in a hotel. Because it is the *patient* who does the therapy. I didn't think it was the family that needed therapy, even though the parents were impatient, the sisters called her bad names, the schoolchildren ridiculed her. My feeling was that her parents would have to adjust to her dry beds. So would her sisters and the schoolchildren—and the neighbors. In fact, I saw no other course for them. I didn't think it was necessary to explain anything to the father, the mother, the sisters, or anybody else. I had told her what she already knew but didn't know that she knew.

And all of you have grown up with the idea that when you empty your bladder you empty it all the way. And you assume that. The important thing is that all of you have had the experience of being interrupted and shutting off a stream of urine very suddenly. Everybody has that experience—and she had forgotten it. All I did was remind her of something she already knew but didn't know she knew it.

In other words, in doing therapy you regard your patient as an individual and no matter how much of a problem her bedwetting was to her parents, her sisters, neighbors and school children, it was primarily *her* problem. And all she needed to know was something she already knew—and the therapy for all the others was letting them make their own adjustments.

Psychotherapy should be an orientation to the patient and an orientation to the primary problem itself. And remember this. That all of us have our individual language, and that when you listen to a patient, you should listen knowing that he is speaking an alien language and that you should not try to understand in terms of your language. Understand the patient in *his* language.

This is one of my favorite Erickson tales, perhaps because Erickson would almost always introduce it with a comment such as "You will be especially interested in this story, Sid." I puzzled for a long time before I could find his message to me and finally was able to extract two main ones.

The first is that I can learn control of thoughts, of working energies, and of symptoms, such as anxiety. I must do this, however, not by willpower, but by discovering which stimuli are necessary to induce me to "start and stop." Then I must take the opportunities to practice "starting and stopping."

The second message is that "all of you have grown up with the idea that when you empty your bladder, you empty it all the way." In the version of this tale that was published in A Teaching Seminar with Milton H. Erickson, *edited by Jeffrey Zeig, Erickson added some extra sentences that make this second point even clearer. "All she needed to know was that she could stop her urination at any time, with the* right stimulus." *And, "We grow up thinking that we have got to finish. That isn't true, that we must continue until we are finished." I have found this attitude to be a great help in accomplishing such tasks as writing. The coercive feeling that we must finish can easily block spontaneity and creativity. A far more effective way of getting something done is by "starting and stopping," according to one's inner rhythm. I have found this story to be effective in helping patients overcome blockages, such as writer's block.*

BOLO TIE

All our life we learn to place limits on so many things. I can think of Bill Folsey, a KOOL–TV newsman. On a trip to Chicago he went to a restaurant, where the headwaiter informed him that he would have to wear a tie—and not that bolo tie that Bill was wearing. Bill asked the headwaiter, "What did you pay for *your* tie?"

The waiter said, very proudly, "Twenty-five dollars."

And Bill said, *"My* tie cost two hundred dollars."

The waiter didn't know what to think. And Bill Folsey walked into the restaurant and took a seat where he *chose* to sit—while the waiter tried to give that some thought. That odd-looking thing that Bill Folsey had on! A two-hundred-dollar tie! While *his* was only a twenty-five-dollar one.

So, have a dream. And, every time you dream, you have the right and the privilege of redreaming that dream, with another cast of characters. And, in that way, you can discover many things you've been trained not to know. Your teachers, a long time ago, told you, "Look at me when you are speaking to me. Look at me when I'm speaking to you." And you learned, *"Don't* do this, and *don't* do that. Wear the *right* clothes, the right shoes. Tie your shoe strings *right."* So much of our learning is based upon limited instructions that bar us from our own development of our understanding—and we get into patterns of being limited.

I taught my sons how to hoe a potato patch—by making designs. And all the time they are making designs with their hoes and hoeing the potato patch, they are wondering what their last design will be. So, my sons learned to hoe a potato patch by hoeing triangles, and more and more triangles, and, on their own, they discovered that they could hoe circles and numbers, and letters.

And it is wonderful, to have a night's sleep, a sound and restful sleep—and not find out until next week that you have dreamed that night. You didn't know about that dream—until a week later.

The comments that Erickson made after the tale of the bolo tie might seem to be irrelevant. Actually, they are his way of repeating and driving home the main points in his tale. The first point is that we are limited in our patterns of understanding and action. ("Wear the right clothes . . . So much of our learning is based upon limited instructions.") The second point is that we can replace our limited, and limiting, instructions with new patterns—of our own devising ("circles and numbers, and letters"). Finally, Erickson frames his comments with the suggestion that

*the listener should discover new patterns in a dream. He should
trust his unconscious mind to devise novel ways of overcoming
habitual limitations.*

SIN

A young woman came to see me. She was brought up to
believe that theaters are places where young girls are seduced and
places of sin. She would not go into a drugstore, because they sold
tobacco there and the Lord might strike her to the ground if she
was in a place that dispensed tobacco. And she wouldn't drink
wine or cider or any alcoholic beverage, because, if she did, God
would strike her dead. God would strike her dead if she went to
the theater; he'd strike her dead if she smoked a cigarette.

I inquired about her employment. She worked for a doctor
who belonged to her church. He paid her $100 a month. The
average salary at that time was $270 a month. She had worked
for him for ten years and she was still getting just $100 a month.
And her typewriting speed was no higher than twenty-five words
a minute.

She lived at home with her parents, who guarded their daughter very carefully—against sin. It took her an hour to get to work,
eight hours of work, sometimes overtime without pay. It took her
another hour to get home. And she worked six days a week. She
went to church on Sunday—all day long. It was a very rigid and
limited family.

When the girl left my office after the first interview, my wife,
who seldom comments on patients, said, "Who was that thing
that the cat dragged in?"

I said, "Just a patient of mine."

So I talked to the girl and I persuaded her that life is full of
pitfalls and death comes to all and if it was God's plan for her to
die at a certain time, I was certain that she would not die of

smoking cigarettes, unless God was ready to receive her. I got her to smoke a cigarette. She coughed a lot and God did not strike her dead! He really didn't! That surprised her.

Then I suggested that she go to the theater. It took a couple of weeks to build up her courage. She told me, very earnestly, "God will strike me dead if I go to a house of sin."

I told her that if God did not strike her dead it would be because it was not her time to die and that I had great doubts about it being her time to die. Would she please come and tell what movie she had seen? She returned after seeing *The Lady and the Tramp*. I didn't pick out that movie.

She said, "The church must be wrong. There wasn't a *thing* bad in that movie. There weren't any corrupting men despoiling young girls. I think the movie was entertaining."

I said, "I think the church has given you a false idea about movies. I don't think the church did it intentionally. I think the church did it out of ignorance." And she found other movies interesting—especially musicals. Then one day I told her, "I think you've improved enough to take a drink of whiskey."

She said, "God will surely strike me dead."

I said, "I have doubts about it. He didn't strike you dead when you went to the theater or when you smoked a cigarette. Let's see if he strikes you dead if you take a drink of whiskey."

She took a drink of whiskey and waited and waited and God didn't strike her dead. Then she said, "I think I've got to make some changes in my life. I think I had better move out of my parents' home and get an apartment of my own."

I said, "And you need to get a better job. You need to learn how to type. And move into an apartment of your own. You can't afford it, so feel free to ask your parents to pay for the apartment. And do your own cooking and rent a typewriter. As soon as you awaken in the morning you rush to the typewriter, the very first thing, and type, 'This is a beautiful day in June.' Then you go to the bathroom, brush your teeth, and type another brief sentence, typing full speed for each sentence. Make each sentence very short. Then start dressing. Halfway through dressing, type another sentence. When you finish dressing, type another short sentence. Start getting your breakfast ready and type another short sentence. Sit down to eat, and halfway through breakfast get up and type a short sentence—always typing at top speed. You can do that interrupted practice, always at full speed, and you will learn to type at a much more rapid rate."

In three months time she was up to a speed of eighty words a minute.

As for her cooking, she said, "I thought I'd make some rice and I figured I could heat a cup of rice. I put it in a pan with water. Then I had to get another pan because the cup of rice filled that big pan. And I had to get a couple of other pans. I didn't know rice swelled like that."

I said, "There's a lot of things to learn about cooking."

I had her bake some beans. She measured that cup of beans very carefully and they swelled into an enormous quantity. She eventually became a good cook and she resigned from her church and told her parents, "I'll come to visit you now and then. I've got a good job now. It's $270 a month and I only have to walk eight blocks to get to my job."

Then she came to me and about that time Mrs. Erickson said to me, "Milton, do you specialize in beautiful blonds?"

I said, "The cat dragged in that last one." Because that girl turned out to be very pretty. She took music lessons and enjoyed her work.

Then she came to me after some months and said, "Dr. Erickson, I want to get drunk and I want to know how to do it."

I said, "The best way of getting drunk is to give me a promise that you will not use the telephone, that you will lock your door and not unlock it, and that you will remain in your apartment.

Get a bottle of wine and enjoy drinking it, sip by sip, until you have got the entire bottle drunk."

She came to me within the next few days and said, "I'm glad you made me promise not to use the phone, because I wanted to call up all my friends and invite them to come over and get drunk with me. And that would have been terrible. And I wanted to go out into the street and sing. And I promised you that I would lock the door and wouldn't unlock it. I'm so glad you made me promise. You know, getting drunk was fun, but I had a bad headache the next morning. I don't think I want to get drunk again."

I said, "For the joy of getting drunk you have to pay a bill, and that is a headache—a hangover. And you are at liberty to have as many hangovers as you want."

She said, "I don't want any more hangovers."

She later got married. Now I've lost track of her.

I think it's very important to take the patient seriously and meet his wishes. Not to exercise cold, hard judgment. And recognize that people need to learn things, that you really aren't competent to teach them all the things they need. That they can learn a lot on their own. And that she certainly did. And they are usually marvelously polite in a trance.

Get them to break prohibitions! This is one of Erickson's prime rules for treating many types of symptom complexes, including, of course, phobias and inhibitory states. First, in the outlining of the history, Erickson is careful to elicit signs of limitations, rigidities, narrow "sets." Then, using the patients' own beliefs, he will set about getting them to break the prohibitions.

Here, Erickson presents a situation of a young woman who is extremely limited. Her limitations are seen as coming from her rigid church and family teachings. Of course, they could just as easily come from inner strictures. His prime method of helping her to break her prohibitions, to extend her world experiences, and to build her ability to live independently and self-sufficiently is to induce her to put herself into new situations. In these new situations she learns, from her own experience, not from the dictates of others, what her limitations actually are. She also learns something about dealing with materials, such as rice.

Of course, Erickson, typically, in talking about the expansion of the rice and of the beans, seeds universal ideas about expansion. In fact, the whole story can be seen as illustrating the expansion of a very small personality into a much larger one. Her income expands from $100 per month to $270 per month. Her personality blooms and her looks manifest this, so that she changes from "something that the cat dragged in" to "beautiful blond." And the patient does find out her own limitations—from experience. For example, she learns from the experience of having a hangover. Finally, Erickson gives a hint as to how he gets people to do things that they would not ordinarily consider doing. He explains, "They are usually marvelously polite in a trance."

In putting emphasis on impulses and feeling over intellect and concepts, Erickson is merely trying to correct for the imbalance that develops in most people. As he told me once, "In a child the body tries to keep up with the feet. In an adult, the feet try to keep up with the body (and head)."

REDUCE—GAIN—REDUCE

A woman came to see me and she said, "I weigh 180 pounds. I've dieted successfully under doctors' orders hundreds of times. And I want to weigh 130 pounds. Every time I get to 130 pounds I rush into the kitchen to celebrate my success. I put it back on, right away. Now I weigh 180. Can you use hypnosis to help me reduce to 130 pounds? I'm back to 180 for the hundredth time."

I told her, yes, I could help her reduce by hypnosis, but she wouldn't like what I did.

She said she wanted to weigh 130 pounds and she didn't care what I did.

I told her she'd find it rather painful.

She said, "I'll do anything you say."

I said, "All right. I want an absolute promise from you that you will follow my advice exactly."

She gave me the promise very readily and I put her into a trance. I explained to her again that she wouldn't like my method of reducing her weight and would she promise me, absolutely, that she would follow my advice? She gave me that promise.

Then I told her, "Let both your unconscious mind and your conscious mind listen. Here's the way you go about it. Your present weight is now 180 pounds. I want you to gain twenty pounds and when you weigh 200 pounds, on my scale, you may start reducing."

She literally begged me, on her knees, to be released from her promise. And every ounce she gained she became more and more insistent on being allowed to start reducing. She was markedly distressed when she weighed 190 pounds. When she was 190 she begged and implored to be released from her own promise. At 199 she said that was close enough to 200 pounds and I insisted on 200 pounds.

When she reached 200 pounds she was very happy that she could begin to reduce. And when she got to 130 she said, "I'm never going to gain again."

Her pattern had been to reduce and gain. I reversed the pattern and made her gain and reduce. And she was very happy with the final results and maintained that weight. She didn't want to, ever again, go through that horrible agony of gaining twenty pounds.

For this patient, the gaining of weight is no longer either rebellion or an expression of something she wants to do. It has become something she has been coerced into doing. Therefore, just as she had previously resented having to lose weight, she now resents having to gain weight.

In "Sin," Erickson illustrated that sometimes it is necessary to help the patient to "break the prohibition." Here he shows that it is often helpful to get patients to change their pattern. In this case, he simply had the woman reverse her pattern of reducing and gaining. Once she had done this she could no longer go through the same sequence repeatedly, as she had done all her life. She apparently had learned to be able to tolerate gaining weight only up to 180 pounds. We see this in many weight patients. They have a level of tolerance, at which point they urgently feel the need to reduce. Erickson succeeded in making this tolerance level intolerable because he made her go beyond it.

This method of reversing patterns or looking at things in a reverse way is one of Erickson's favorite approaches for changing mental sets. He liked to show patients a book called Topsys & Turvys, *by Peter Newell, in which the stories and the illustrations change meaning when the book is turned upside down.*

A GORGEOUS WAY TO DIET

Now, another girl was overweight, and markedly so. I pointed out to her, "You're overweight and you've dieted and dieted, to no avail. And you tell me that you can stay on a diet for a week, or two weeks, even three weeks, and then you fall off and gorge. Then you're despairing and gorge some more.

"Now, I'll give you a medical prescription. Continue the diet given to you by your doctor in the past. Stay on that diet for two weeks and three weeks, if you can. And then, on the last Sunday of that third week, gorge like hell, because it's medical orders. You can't gorge enough to offset your losses in the three weeks. And you can gorge without a sense of guilt because you're under medical orders to gorge all day Sunday. And the following Monday go back to your diet. Stay on it three weeks, if you can, and then have another guiltless gorge day."

In my last letter from her she says that there has to be a better way to diet than saving up her hunger three weeks. She wants to be hungry each day, wants to enjoy food and enjoy the proper amount, each day. The gorging days gave her the strength to be on the diet for those three weeks.

This approach falls into the category of "prescribing the symptom." Erickson told the patient to do exactly what she had been doing—dieting for three weeks, "when she was able," and then gorging. All that changed was the length of time devoted to the gorging. If a pattern can be changed, even in some small way, there is the possibility for further change. As we have seen many times, this is one of Erickson's basic approaches in therapy—to initiate a small change.

SIGHT-SEEING

A woman said she wanted me to do something about her weight. I looked at her fingernails. She had long, red fingernails. I think they're advertised as "Nails." You glue them on. They stick out. That amount of fat and those red fingernails!

I said, "I can help you, but you'll have to cooperate. You climb Squaw Peak."

She said, "At sunrise?"

I said, "Yes."

She said, "Well, I'd like some company."

I said, "You complain that your sixteen-year-old son is about a hundred pounds overweight. Take him along for company. Set a good example for him."

Next time I saw her she said, "You know, I don't believe I want to lose weight and I know my son doesn't. Do you mind if I stop trying to fool myself?"

I said, "Not at all."

Another woman called me up and said, "I'm ashamed to come in to see you. For the last two years I've neglected my husband, my family, my children. I've sat in the kitchen and eaten everything I could lay my hands on. My husband takes the children to school and brings them back. He does all the shopping and I cook and eat things. I'm grossly overweight. I don't even want you to be able to see me."

I said, "You want to lose the weight. You've neglected your children and your husband for two years. In that case why don't you take your children out of school? They won't lose anything by it. Your husband's income is sufficient for you to have a car of your own. Take your children out of school; put them in the station wagon and sightsee all over Arizona, New Mexico, Utah, California, and every other cotton-pickin' place you can think of. And make your kids read brochures, historical and geographical brochures, on your sight-seeing trip. Stay in motels where you can't take charge of the kitchen. You'll be too busy looking after your kids to eat. On your husband's present income, he can join you every weekend. The family can really enjoy a vacation for a year."

A year later she called up and said, "I'm back to normal weight. I'm interested in my kids. I love my husband and I want to return to my household duties. Do I have to do any more sight-seeing?"

I said, "Not until you gain weight."

She said, "Don't worry, Doctor. I've had my fill. Now I want to watch my kids grow and I want to look after my home. Motels are deadly. The kids enjoyed them, but *I* have a right to be home. I'm going to protect that right."

I never got a fee out of her and I never met her. But therapy was done on the entire family without my even seeing them. When you touch the vital spot in your patient, your patient either is going to respond and get better or not.

We have just seen three different ways in which Erickson handled problems of overweight. In each case, he found a different area on which to focus his attention and the attention of the patient. Of course, in all three successful cases, the element of motivation was important, and he determined this in the beginning. In the case of the woman who was not motivated, this was also easily determined when she would not follow the simple suggestion of climbing Squaw Peak. Erickson had already guessed that she was lazy and self-indulgent when he saw her general demeanor, which included the ostentatious, artificial fingernails.

In the next two tales the element of motivation is also of central importance.

YOUR ALCOHOLIC HAS TO BE SINCERE

A very wealthy man came to see me and said, "I'm an alcoholic. I want to quit."

I said, "Well, there are a few things I'd like to know about you. Are you married?"

He said, "Yes, very much married."

"What do you mean, 'very much married'?"

"Well, we own a summer cottage, ten miles from nowhere. It's a beautiful place. I could afford to have it fixed up beautifully. My wife and I often spend two or three weeks there. We can catch trout from a trout stream by putting our poles out the bedroom window. There's no telephone. We're ten miles from civilization. It's beautifully furnished. Every kind of food and booze that can be bought is there. And every summer my wife and I spend about three, two or three weeks there in the nude, really enjoying life."

I said, "All right, it will be very easy for you to cease to be an alcoholic. Have your wife drive up to the cabin, collect all the booze, and put it in the car. Put your clothes in the car too. Remove any other clothes that are there and bring them back to Phoenix.

"She can have a friend drive her up there at night and she can turn over all her clothes to her friend. And the two of you can have a delightful two weeks, three weeks, living on trout and being free of booze. I know you won't walk over the desert for ten miles to get a bottle of booze."

He said, "Doctor, I think I'm mistaken about wanting to quit drinking."

But that would have been the perfect way. And your alcoholic has to be sincere.

In his use of the phrase "your alcoholic," Erickson is under-lining his belief that a therapist, once having accepted a patient, assumes a great deal of responsibility for that patient's progress. If you, as a therapist, accept an alcoholic as a patient, he becomes "your alcoholic." Since the man in this story refused to follow Erickson's prescription, he was not accepted as a patient and remained his own alcoholic.

A FRIENDLY DIVORCE

Here's a case where I saw the husband only once. And that's because I got sick. I couldn't see anybody for two months.

A husband came to me and he said, "I'm an only child. My

father's a minister in a very narrow Christian church. I've been brought up to think that smoking is a sin, going to the theater is a sin. In fact, I've been brought up on sin. There's very little you *can* do. I've been careful in medical school not to commit a sin. I met the only daughter of another minister of the same Christian sect, and she's been brought up in the same way that I was. We fell in love. Our parents were delighted and they planned a wonderful wedding for us. They chipped in to pay for our honeymoon in the same hotel that one set of parents had had their honeymoon in. It was 142 miles away from where we lived.

"It was midwinter in Indiana and the temperature was below zero. We had an evening wedding and a nice reception afterwards. Somewhere about ten, eleven o'clock my wife and I got in the car and headed for that hotel, 142 miles away. By the time we got two miles away the heater in the car broke down and when we arrived at that hotel 142 miles away I practically froze. We were miserable, and we were tired. The car had broken down and I didn't know if I would be able to fix it. I also had to change the spare tire.

"When we got there we went up to our room and I opened the door. We stood there looking at each other.

"We both knew what we had to do, but we were so tired, so miserable, so cold. My wife settled it. She picked up her suitcase, turned on the bathroom light, and turned off the light in the main room. She undressed in the bathroom, turned off the light, and came out in her pajamas. She found her way through the darkness to the bed and crawled in.

"So, I picked up my suitcase, went into the bathroom, turned the lights on, got into my pajamas, turned the lights back off, and then found my way through the darkness to the other side of the bed. And we lay there. We knew what we had to do, but we weren't trying to figure anything out except how to get over being cold, miserable, and tired.

"We lay there all night trying to get some sleep, trying to make up our minds.

"Finally, by eleven o'clock in the morning we mustered up enough courage to consummate the marriage, and neither of us enjoyed it. During that first intercourse she became pregnant. We have tried to learn to make love to each other since then, but it's too late. We talked it over, and as soon as she delivers the baby, next month, after her six-weeks checkup, we're going to get a friendly divorce. I don't want to be as stupid about the divorce as I was about the marriage. We both regret the way our marriage turned out. I'm going to give her the baby and child support. They'll go back home. I don't know where I'll go."

I said, "All right. That *is* such a miserable marriage and you've failed to adjust to it. It's complicated by a pregnancy. I suggest you get a friendly divorce. Now let me explain to you how you do it."

I told him, "Go down into Detroit and make arrangements for a private dining room and for a room in a hotel. Hire a nurse to look after your child after your wife's six-week checkup. Explain to your wife that it's time to set out to have a friendly divorce and there ought to be a friendly separation. You take her to the Hotel Statler; I don't care what it costs. Have a private dining room and a wonderful dinner, with candles, and, this is a medical order, a bottle of champagne. And you both share in drinking that champagne.

"After you finish dinner—it should not be later than ten o'clock—go to the desk and get the key to your room. The bellboy will take you there. When you get to your floor, hand the bellboy a five-dollar bill and tell him to scram. He'll know what you mean. Then you walk to your hotel room, unlock the door, pick your bride up, carry her across the threshhold, lock the door while she is still in your arms, and walk over and sit her down on the side of the bed. Then tell her, 'I'll have one last good-bye kiss.' Kiss her gently and remark, 'That kiss was for you, now let's have one for me.' Drop your hand onto her knee, prolong that kiss a little bit, slide your hand and slip off her slipper. Then tell her, 'Let's have one more kiss for the *two* of us.' You slip your hand under her dress, slide your hand down, and take off her other slipper. Then, with the champagne and your endocrine glands and hers, things'll start to shape up. Unzip her blouse and kiss her again. Take off one stocking, kiss her again."

I gave him a complete outline on how to seduce his wife. By summer I had recovered from my illness and both of them had disappeared. Some years later I was lecturing at Emory University. A young man said, "We'd very much like to have you dine with us."

I said, "I'm sorry, my plane ticket makes it impossible."

He said, "She'll be very disappointed."

I wondered why a strange family would be disappointed.

He said, "You look as if you don't recognize me."

I said, "That's right, I don't."

He said, "You undoubtedly remember a dinner you recommended for my wife and myself at the Statler Hotel in Detroit."

I said, "Yes, I do."

He said, "We now have two children and a third on the way."

When people come to you wanting a divorce, maybe they don't.

The couple in this tale are similar, in many ways, to the young woman in "Sin." Because of their rigid, constricting upbringing, they require very clear directive guidance in overcoming their learned limitations. They are also sufficiently respectful of authority to follow such a directive approach. But, we may wonder, "Why does Erickson tell this story to us? We are certainly sophisticated enough to know how to seduce a woman. Is there, perhaps, some secret message in the story?"

*Of course there is. There are many messages. The most obvi-
ous one is that, once again, your best chance of enabling someone
to change his responses is to tell him to do what he already is
doing or, as in this case, is planning to do. Then you inject some
difference, such as a change of scene and atmosphere. You don't
hesitate to give directions or supply information. (If you are the
subject you get relevant information.)*

*The main point of this story is Erickson's belief that we all
have the capacity and resources within us to resolve problems and
differences. Sometimes all we need is the stimulus of a slight
change.*

START THE BALL ROLLING

Now, a twelve-year-old girl is not a child. I had one on whom
I illustrated a purely childish technique. She called me up on the
phone and said, "I had infantile paralysis and I have forgotten
how to move my arms. Can you hypnotize me and teach me?"

I told her mother to bring her over and her mother brought
her over. I looked at the girl. For a twelve-year-old girl she had
a very well developed bust, except that the right breast was under
her arm. I had the mother strip the girl to her waist and I looked
over her entire torso to see what the muscles were.

I told her that three times a day she ought to sit in front of
a mirror, nude to the waist, and make faces at herself.

Now, will you draw down the corner of both sides of your
mouth?

Now, do it again and feel the skin of your chest move. I can
do it on only one side of my face.

And I told her to sit in front of a mirror three times a day,
twenty minutes, and draw down the corners of her mouth. In
other words, contract the platysma muscle.

And she asked me, "Do I have to sit in front of a mirror?"
I said, "Where would you like to sit?"
She said, "I'd like to imagine a TV program."
And so she was watching an imaginary program on an imaginary TV. And she started exercising the platysma muscles, and she enjoyed watching the imaginary TV while making faces.

Now, when you start one muscle moving there's a tendency for that to spread to other muscles. You *try* to move just one finger. You start to spread the movement, unintentionally. Her arms began to move.

Now, the right breast migrated from under her arm to one side of her chest. She is now a lawyer, practicing law.

Erickson's comments about this case are sufficiently explanatory. Again he initiates a small change, apparently quite peripheral to the target problem, which was inability to move the arms. He simply uses his knowledge of anatomy indirectly, to cause the patient to contract her chest muscles, which of course are connected to the arms (especially the pectoralis major). Why didn't he simply tell the girl to practice using her arm muscles? He knew that she had developed too much resistance, which would make such a direct approach useless. But how could she resist such an indirect approach?

CLAUSTROPHOBIA

Another patient had claustrophobia. She couldn't bear to be shut up in a small room. Her mother had punished her as a child by putting her in the outdoor entrance to the cellar, closing the door, and then clicking her heels as she walked down the street, deserting the girl. She had clicked her heels on the sidewalk, making the girl think she was going far, far away.

And the girl grew up with an absolute phobia for small rooms. So I asked her to sit in the closet of my office.

She said, "I'll only do that if the door's wide open."

I said, "Suppose instead of having the door wide open it lacks one millimeter of being wide open?"

And she agreed. She stayed in the closet with the door wide open, except for one millimeter. And then we worked up to two millimeters, three millimeters, a centimeter, half an inch, an inch. And how open did she have to have that door?

So she stood in the closet and slowly closed the door. I waited to see when her panic would develop. She found she was comfortable even when the door was only a half an inch open and she kept her hand on the door knob. Finally she closed it and found out she could live and breathe in that closet with the door closed, as long as she had the doorknob in her hand.

Then I suggested she might try looking through the keyhole. Since she could see outside through the keyhole, she didn't have to hang on to the doorknob any longer.

Claustrophobia is a syndrome that graphically expresses the limitations that have developed in a person. There are many theories about the cause of this and other phobias, but Erickson does not concern himself with them. His concern is to help the sufferer eliminate his stifling feeling of constriction, to move beyond his phobic limitations.

Erickson is telling us to deal with difficult problems bit by bit —first imagine, then gradually close one door. Then do the same with another door, with a window . . .

THE STARS ARE THE LIMIT

A professor of astronomy came in to see me during the winter. He left the front door open. He left my office door open and opened the two other doors in my office.

He opened the shades to one window. He rolled up the blind, pulled up the shade, and opened the window.

He said, "I've been picked by the government to photograph the total eclipse in Borneo and I suffer from claustrophobia. "To get to Borneo I've got to fly, and ride on a train. I've got to travel by ship, by motorcar. I've got to be able to work in a darkroom. Can you fix me up? I've got two months before I have to leave."

So I had him imagine that one of the doors was closed, even though it was actually wide open. Finally he managed to imagine that while under hypnosis. I then had him imagine that the other door was closed, that the window was closed, and that the front door to the office was closed.

He went to Borneo to photograph the total eclipse of the sun.

After he had succeeded, in a trance state, in imagining that the door was closed, I actually closed it, just a little bit at a time, until it finally was closed. One by one I closed every door, after first having him imagine it was closed. And it all started by having him imagine that the door was closed. I'd called that open door a crack in the wall. I said, "Now let's close that crack, a bit at a time, into a solid wall."

Now, if you had claustrophobia, you'd want the windows open and the doors open. I'd put you in a trance and have you see a wide crack here. And, no matter how bad your claustrophobia was, you could stand sitting on that couch with all the windows open and that door open. And, when I alter the mental picture that you have, you'll relate to it the way you do to the wall behind you.

And that's the advantage of hypnosis. You can have people in a trance state imagine effectively that such and such a doorway is actually a crack in a wall. And they will have a wall behind them. Now, the windows and doors must be open. When they change into cracks in the wall, slowly close the cracks.

After he got to Borneo and photographed the eclipse, the man entered his darkroom and developed pictures. Because he desperately wanted to see the land of Borneo, or wherever it was.

The next winter his wife came to see me and said, "Thank goodness this winter I won't have to sleep with all the doors and all the windows open."

In this claustrophobia case Erickson again helps the patient gradually to tolerate more and more "closedness." While the desensitization was done in actuality in the first case, it was first done in fantasy in the case of the astronomy professor. The fantasy experience was then confirmed when Erickson actually closed the doors. Erickson not only closes actual doors, after first leaving them open, but he also, via hypnotic suggestion, produces a "wide crack" in a solid wall. He demonstrates that he can take over control of the patient's phobic feelings as well as his perceptions—by producing and removing such visual hallucinations. He ties in the hallucination of the wide crack with a feeling of openness—associated with "you could stand sitting on that couch with all the windows open and that door open." Then, when he "alters the mental picture," he can suggest that the feeling of safety and comfort will remain, even after the "wide crack" is removed.

BLOOD ON THE KEYS

A doctor had two sons and a daughter. He decided that the older son, Henry, was to be a doctor. The mother decided that this son would be a concert pianist. For four hours each day she made him practice the piano. The father didn't see anything wrong with this. Henry soon learned that he had to outwit his mother in some way. So he bit his fingernails down to the quick, and as he played the piano he left traces of blood all over the keys. His mother was hardhearted, and she made him play in spite of that. He bit his nails more, but no amount of blood interfered with his practice. He kept on biting his nails. He was not allowed to go to school unless he played the piano four hours a day. And he wanted to go to school. Later, he wanted to go to high school. So he had to practice the piano four hours a day. Later, when he wanted to go to college, he had to practice four hours a day to get his allowance.

After college, Henry's father wanted him to go to medical school and Henry didn't want to do this. He managed to flunk out of medical school. His father was a good politician and got him admitted to another medical school. He flunked out of that school. By this time Henry had his own ideas. He wanted to study political science, so he deliberately cheated, openly, brazenly cheated, and he was blacklisted from all medical schools. His father brought him to me and told me, "Hypnotize him and make him stop biting his nails."

Henry was twenty-six. Henry said, "I want to study political science but my father left me without any funds."

Henry got a job with a mortician. He hated it. He drove an ambulance there. And I told the father, "I'll take care of your son. I have my own ways of doing therapy."

The father said, "I don't care about your ways of doing therapy as long as you make Henry grow his nails. There is no way I can get my son into medical school with those horrible fingers."

I said to Henry, "What do you think about your habit?"

Henry said, "It's an ingrown pattern of mine. I can't help biting my nails. I must do it in my sleep. I have no desire to have nails like this. They're hideous! I would not like to have a pretty girl look at my hands."

I said, "Well, Henry, you have ten fingers. Now, I'm absolutely positive that nine fingers can furnish you with all the nail diet you need and you can grow a long nail on any given finger while you feed on the other nine."

Henry said, "That's right."

I said, "In fact, you could have two fingers to grow long nails and the other eight could furnish you all the nail diet you want."

Henry said, "I see exactly what you are getting at. It will end up with your telling me *one* finger is all I need to feed on and I can grow nine finger nails. And, dammit, I'm *caught* with your logic!" It didn't take him long to grow ten fingernails.

Then I said, "Henry, your father is not supporting you. You are working, and you play the piano four hours a day."

He said, "I like music but I hate the piano. I really like music."

I said, "A piano isn't the only instrument. You've had twenty-two years of experience of playing on instruments' keys."

Henry said, "I'll get me an electric organ."

And he played the electric organ so perfectly that he was very much in demand for weddings and parties. And he played the electric organ all the way through law school. His father was furious at me!

The second son, the father had decided, was to become an Episcopalian priest. That son had married a Jewish woman. And he'd gotten a job in a second-hand-car lot. He was a drunkard, selling second-hand cars, and married to a Jewish woman!

And the daughter had *her* instructions. She was to grow up and become a charge nurse. And the daughter ran away at sixteen. She went to one of the Carolinas and married her teenage sweetheart.

Henry's brother decided that if Henry could study political science and law, he and his Jewish wife did not have to keep on hating each other. They were both unhappy with the marriage. He didn't have to keep on drinking. He divorced her. Episcopalian ministers are not supposed to be divorced. He said, "You can't make an Episcopalian minister out of me—and I'm going to be a car dealer. I'm going to deal in *new* cars!" And he succeeded in that!

And Henry, the lawyer, and his brother, the car dealer, laid down the law for the sister and her sixteen-year-old husband. They visited both sets of parents and laid down the law. Her husband was to go to college and get good marks. He could study anything he pleased. And the sister was to go to college and get a bachelor's degree and she and her husband could make their own joint decisions.

In this tale, the coercive nature of the parents is highlighted. The father had a fixed idea that his son must be a doctor. The mother had a fixed idea that her son must become a pianist. Typically, the father ordered Erickson to "hypnotize him and make him stop biting his nails." Even after Henry had been blacklisted from all medical schools, the father blindly insisted that it was only his bitten nails that prevented Henry from being accepted in another medical school. For many years Henry had reacted to his parents' coercion with symptoms such as nail biting. Of course, he did not feel that he was responsible for his symptoms. He said, "I can't help biting my nails." Let's look at how Erickson dealt with him—and with his entire family.

Erickson intervened at first by taking responsibility on himself, presenting himself as "a good father." He said, "I will take care of your son." He then showed himself to be a more rational guide with whom the son could identify, without delaying his own legitimate wishes and strivings. By the use of a double bind (telling him to bite, but not bite), he got Henry to admit very early in therapy, "I am caught in your logic." Henry could see that if he followed Erickson's suggestion, he could satisfy any nail-biting needs while allowing most of his nails to grow. In other words, he was encouraged to express any legitimate impulses, but to direct them—in this case, to one fingernail. Next, Erickson applied this principle to the question of playing the piano. He determined that Henry did enjoy music and encouraged him to express and satisfy this area of interest and enjoyment. However, Henry selected his own instrument. Once he had discovered that he could do what he wanted to do, he was able to go further in determining his own path in life and work himself through law school by utilizing the talent and interest he had already developed.

After Henry had broken away from the imprisoning influence of his parents and had found more effective methods of rebelling than nail biting, he was able to help his brother to assert himself. The two brothers then joined forces to "lay down the law" to their parents and, in fact, to the entire family, including their sister's young husband and his parents. They were able to do this because they had the strength of numbers and unity and because they now represented rational values and "healthy" goals. Interestingly, they did not insist that the sister leave her sixteen-year-old husband. The husband, instead, was included in the self-betterment program that had always been a family priority and that was, incidentally, important to Erickson.

The mother and father obviously believed in education and self-improvement. Unfortunately, they had been too rigid and insensitive in their attempts to impose their values on their children. Finally, though, all the children were able to satisfy their parents' healthy concern for them. Henry became a professional, a lawyer, and an organist, thus satisfying both his father's and his mother's hopes. Henry's brother dissolved the mixed marriage that undoubtedly distressed his parents and succeeded as a new-car dealer. The sister acquired a college education.

Erickson illustrates the "ripple effect," as described by Spiegel. This effect is seen in each individual and through the family. Alleviation of Henry's nail biting led to greater self-confidence, which led to Henry's assertive behavior. He "selected his own instrument." The freeing of one member of the family from irrational coercion led to the freeing of the next, which led to the freeing of the next. Even the overly anxious parents were undoubtedly freed from their undue concern about their children. In any therapy, we know that although we are focusing on one patient, any changes in that patient will affect and change everyone in his "world" or "system."

6. Reframing

There are many examples of the reframing process in the literature of psychotherapy. One of the most memorable is Victor Frankl's account of being in a concentration camp in his book From Death-Camp to Existentialism. While most of his fellow inmates lost hope and subsequently died, Frankl occupied his mind thinking about the lectures he would give after his release —lectures that would draw on his experiences in the camp. Thus, he reframed the potentially deadening and hopeless situation. He transformed it in his mind to a source of rich experiences that he could use to help others overcome apparently hopeless situations —physical or mental. Of course, there are skeptics who would say that this type of thinking had no effect on his subsequent survival; or that hopelessness did not necessarily condemn the inmates to death. Be that as it may, that type of thinking certainly kept his spirits and his mind alive at that time. And, it may also have kept his body alive. Again, we note that Frankl's reframing was syntonic with his general orientation to life. He did value teaching and he had experiences with lecturing, so that it was natural for him to use this experience as source material for lectures in the future.

Watzlawick, Weakland, and Fisch, in Change, say: "To reframe means to change the conceptual and/or emotional setting or viewpoint in relation to which a situation is experienced and to place it in another frame which fits the 'facts' of the same concrete situation equally well, or even better, and thereby changes its entire meaning."

These authors quote the philosopher Epictetus as saying, "It is not the things themselves which trouble me, but the opinions that we have about these things." They point out that "our experience of the world is based on the categorization of the objects of our perception into classes," and that "once an object is conceptualized as the member of a given class, it is extremely difficult to see it also as belonging to another class." With reframing, once we see "alternative class memberships," it is difficult to go back to our previously limited view of "reality."

The following tales provide examples of ways in which Erickson used reframing.

RAISING THEIR BIGNESS

My son, Robert, had put a second story on his home. The night before, he and his wife had moved upstairs. Little five-year-old Douglas and two-year-old Becky were terribly afraid because they had to be left downstairs. Robert came to me. So I advised Robert, "Douglas's bed is lower than the parental bed." Robert was to stress how big a boy he was and relate his bigness to the bigness of the parental bed that was left downstairs. And Becky was to relate her bigness to the bigness of Douglas's bed.

And then I told Robert to make sure the children knew how they could use the intercom from downstairs to upstairs. And they slept beautifully, though Douglas had been very worried. He even had asked if he could sleep upstairs the first few nights.

The important thing was to concentrate on something that emphasized the self, the bigness of the bed, and that he was a big boy.

Erickson appeals to every child's wish to grow up. Robert's children were directed away from their fear and feeling of help-

lessness and toward looking at themselves as becoming bigger.

Instead of looking at what they had lost—the company of their parents—the children were directed toward the future. Douglas was being told that by looking at his parents' bed, he was next in line to fill that bed. Similarly, Becky was reminded that she was growing bigger and would soon fill Douglas's bed.

STYLE

My daughter came home from grade school and said, "Daddy, all the girls in school bite their nails and I want to be in style too."

I said, "Well, you certainly ought to be in style. I think style is very important for girls. You are way behind the girls. They have had a lot of practice. So I think the best way for you to catch up with the girls is to make sure you bite your nails enough each day. Now I think if you bite your nails for fifteen minutes three times a day, every day (I'll furnish a clock) at exactly such-and-such an hour, you can catch up."

She began enthusiastically at first. Then she began beginning late and quitting early and one day she said, "Daddy, I'm going to start a new style at school—long nails."

Starting by "joining the patient" in her desire to be in style, Erickson proceeds to make the "stylish behavior" into an ordeal. He often used this approach to symptoms—making it more of a bother to keep them than to give them up.

THE EASIEST GIRL TO SEDUCE

Now here's a letter from a college student who came to me during her senior year. And she said, "My mother was dominated by her mother all her life. And my mother swore that when she grew up, if she ever had a child, she wouldn't dominate her child. So my mother has been my best pal, my best friend. My mother was my best friend, my pal, all through grade school and through high school. Then I went to California, to a Catholic university there. I am a very ardent Catholic. And my mother calls me twice a week or I call her twice a week and we write letters every week to each other, as she is my best pal.

"But there is something wrong somewhere. When I went to college I went from my normal weight of 105 up to 130 pounds. The first summer I came home I dropped down to 80-odd pounds. Then when I went back to college I went back up to 130 pounds. Next summer I dropped back to 80-odd pounds. And the third summer the same thing happened. Now it's Easter time and I am going to graduate this year. I weigh 130 pounds and I plan to spend the summer in Phoenix. And I can't stand being so fat. I eat junk food all the time, in a compulsive way. Will you help me?"

So I put her into a trance and discussed her weight. And then I found out: the older generation cannot be a pal to a kindergarten student, to a grade-school student.

I told her that her mother wasn't a true pal. The girl hadn't had any boyfriends and she always confided everything to her mother. When she had a boyfriend she would drop him because he gave her funny feelings. She was unable to describe those feelings.

Now, I told her in a trance state that she needed to know certain things, that she could listen to me with her unconscious mind. Then I was going to work with her so that she could listen with her conscious mind. In a light trance state, I explained how a mother can't be a girl's best friend and, to the contrary, that her mother was dominating her in a way opposite to the way *she* had been dominated. I told her she had to think that over until she understood it. I told her we would take up the weight problem later. That summer she came back to Phoenix and only dropped down to 112 pounds. Then she said, "You're right, my mother does dominate me in a reverse way to the way her mother dominates her. And Grandmother lives with us and she dominates Mother and dominates Father. And my father is a drunk. My mother dominates me and I would like to be a normal girl. I know I have funny feelings that I don't understand.

So I told her, "You are an ardent Catholic, you are very devout, but you are the easiest girl in the United States to seduce."

She looked horrified. She said, "Nobody could possibly seduce me."

I said, "I'll explain to you how easily you can be seduced. And you think it over. If I were a young man and wanted to seduce you, I'd ask you for a date, take you out to dinner and to a movie, and show you a most wonderful time. On the second date I would tell you that I thought you were very beautiful and that I had a strong physical attraction to you. And the rest of the date would be absolutely pure. I'd see to it that you had a good time. On the third date I'd tell you that I would really like to seduce you but I know that you are not the kind of girl that can be seduced. 'So I'll just drop the subject and let's have a nice date.' And I would advise you, 'Don't give me eight dates. You'll be perfectly safe with the first seven dates. But don't give me an eighth date.'

"Then it would be safe for you to give me a fourth date, a fifth date, a sixth date. And all the time your hormones would be working on you. On the seventh date your hormones would be well worked up. I would kiss you good-night on the forehead. I'd wait a week and call you for the eighth date. And you know what would happen."

So she agreed about what would happen.

I said, "Now, concerning your weight, you had a bad pattern, of four years' duration. You can't overcome it at once. Now, for next Christmas, I want you to give me a front and mirror view of yourself wearing a bikini. And I want it hand delivered on Christmas day."

She came in with the pictures. She was wretched and miserable. "I weighed 127 pounds when that picture was taken. And I hated myself."

I said, "You certainly are carrying a lot of blubber. Now I don't want to keep these pictures. You can take them back."

She said, "I don't want them either. I'm going to tear them up."

A year later she weighed between 100 and 105 pounds and she had a steady boyfriend. And she said, "His hands stop at my knees —and they stop at my shoulders. I know what those funny feelings are. And I'm not going to teach another year in the Catholic school. I'm going to get a job at the public school."

And so, this September she began teaching at a public school. And she was a very beautiful girl.

Erickson commented that when this student was at home, she was a "little" girl; when she was away from home, she was a "big" girl. He had noted this, but he did not feel that it was necessary for the patient to have this insight. Why is Erickson telling her that she can be seduced? First, he gets her complete attention with this challenge. Then, I believe, he is trying to point out that she has the capacity for normal sexual feelings—that in fact, these "funny feelings" that would cause her to drop a boyfriend were normal sexual feelings. He is letting her experience, in imagination, the way these feelings could be built up to the point where she would really feel them. Her attitude toward those "funny" feelings is reframed. She is able to feel positively about them and to think about them.

After Erickson has "seduced" her with his story, he insists that she bring him a picture of herself in a bikini. By viewing the picture, which reveals her as almost nude, he is consolidating the fantasy of intimacy that he had initiated ("seduction"). Then, as a "big" girl, away from home, she has the experience of a "lover" (Erickson) rejecting her overweight image, by referring to her "blubber" and by saying that he does not want to keep the pictures. She also rejects the overweight image of herself, by tearing up the pictures. As a result of her interaction with Erickson, she has changed her self-image and her attitude about her sexuality.

WALK A MILE

A medically retired policeman told me, "I have emphysema, high blood pressure, and, as you can see, I am grossly overweight. I drink too much. I eat too much. I want a job but my emphysema and high blood pressure prevent that. I would like to cut down on my smoking. I'd like to get rid of it. I'd like to quit drinking about a fifth of whiskey a day and I'd like to eat sensibly."

I said, "Are you married?"

He said, "No, I'm a bachelor. I usually do my own cooking, but there's a handy little restaurant around the corner that I often visit."

"So, there's a handy little restaurant around the corner where you can dine. Where do you buy your cigarettes?"

He bought two cartons at a time. I said, "In other words, you buy cigarettes not for today but for the future. Now, since you do most of your own cooking, where do you shop?"

"Fortunately there is a little grocery right around the corner. That's where I get my groceries and my cigarettes."

"Where do you get your liquor?"

"Fortunately there is a nice liquor store right next to that grocery."

"So, you have a handy restaurant right around the corner, a handy grocery right around the corner, and a handy liquor store right around the corner. And you want to jog and you know you can't jog. Now, your problem is very simple. You want to jog but you can't. But you can walk. All right, buy your cigarettes one pack at a time. Walk across town to buy your pack. That will start to get you in shape. As for your groceries, don't shop at the handy grocery around the corner. Go to a grocery a half mile or a mile away and buy just enough for each meal. That means three nice walks a day. As for your liquor, you can drink all you want to. Take your first drink at a bar at least a mile away. If you want a second drink, find another bar at least a mile away. If you want a third, find another bar a mile away."

He looked at me with the greatest of anger. He swore at me. He left raging.

About a month later a new patient came in. He said, "A retired policemen referred me to you. He said you are the one psychiatrist who knows what he is doing."

The policeman couldn't buy a carton of cigarettes after that! And he knew that walking to the grocery was a conscious act. He had control of it. Now, I didn't take food away from him. I didn't take tobacco away, I didn't take liquor away. I gave him the opportunity to *walk*.

This patient was forced to reframe his behavior. He had to take it out of the category of involuntary behavior. He realized, as Erickson commented, that "walking to the grocery was a conscious act."

Here Erickson recognized that he was dealing with a man who had a long history of carrying out orders. Therefore, he gives him orders with the expectation that the man will carry them out. This is an important example of meeting the patient in his frame of reference. One would not necessarily treat other patients in this manner.

WHISTLEBERRIES

One day a college girl passed flatus loudly in the classroom while writing on the blackboard. And she turned and ran out and went to her apartment, drew the blinds, and ordered her groceries over the telephone and collected them long after dark. And, I got a letter from her saying, "Will you accept me as a patient?"

I noticed the Phoenix address that she gave and I wrote back, "Yes, I would." And she wrote back, "Are you really *sure* you *want* me as a patient?" I wondered about it—and I wrote back, "Yes, I *would* like you."

It took her about three months, and then she wrote me and said, "I would like an appointment with you after dark. And I don't want anybody to see me. Now, please don't have anybody around when I come to your office."

I gave her a ten-thirty appointment, and she told me about passing flatus loudly in the classroom and running out of the room and confining herself to her cabin. She also told me that she was a converted Catholic. Now, converted Catholics are always so ardent; and I questioned her, "Are you *really* a good Catholic?" And she assured me she was. And I spent a couple of hours with her, questioning her about her goodness as a Catholic.

And then in the next interview, I said, "You say you are a good Catholic. Then why do you insult the Lord; why do you make a mockery of him? Because you *are*. You ought to be ashamed of yourself—making a mockery of God and calling yourself a good Catholic!"

She tried to defend herself.

I said, "I can *prove* that you have little respect for God." I hauled out my anatomy book, an atlas, showing all the illustrations of the body. I showed her a cross-section of the rectum and anal sphincter.

I said, "Now, man is very skilled at building things. But, can you imagine a man being sufficiently skillful to build a valve that contains solid matter, liquid matter, and air—and emits downward only the *air?*" I said, "God did. Why don't you *respect* God?"

Then I told her, "Now, I want you to demonstrate earnest, honest respect for God. I want you to bake some beans. They are called whistleberries by the navy. Flavor them with onions and garlic. And get in the nude and prance and dance around your apartment, emitting loud ones, soft ones, big ones, little ones . . . and enjoy God's work."

And she did that. A year later she was married and I made a house call to check up on her. She had a baby. And while I was visiting her, she said, "It's time to nurse the baby." She opened her blouse, exposing her breast, and fed the baby and chatted casually with me. A complete change of reference.

CINNAMON FACE

A woman whom I had treated for pain came to see me. She said, "I'm not seeing you for myself now. I want to see you about my daughter. She is eight years old. She hates her sister; she hates me; she hates her father; she hates her teacher, her schoolmates; hates the mailman, the milkman, the man in the gas station—she just plain hates everybody. She hates herself. I've tried, for a long time, to get her to go to Kansas for the summer to visit her grandparents. She hates them but she doesn't know them."

So I asked, "What's all this hate about?"

"A mass of freckles on her face. The kids in school call her Freckles and she hates those freckles terribly."

I said, "Where is the girl?"

"She's out in the car, doesn't want to come in. She hates *you* because she's got freckles."

I said, "Go out and bring the girl in, even if you have to use force. And bring her into this room."

I sat at my desk in the other room. The mother didn't have to use force. The girl came in and stood in the doorway, her fists clenched, her jaw jutting out, glowering at me and ready for a fight.

As she stood there, I looked at her and said, "You're a thief! You steal!"

She said she was not a thief and she did not steal. She could do battle on that score.

"Oh, yes, *you're* a thief. You steal things. I even know *what* you stole. I even have *proof* that you stole."

She said, "You haven't got proof. I never stoled nothin'.'"

I said, "I even know *where* you were when you stoled what you stole."

That girl was thoroughly angry with me. I said, "I'll tell you where you were and what you stole. You were in the kitchen, setting the kitchen table. You were standing at the kitchen table. You were reaching up to the cookie jar, containing cinnamon cookies, cinnamon buns, cinnamon rolls—and you spilled some cinnamon on your face—you're a Cinnamon Face."

That was two years ago.

What she did was react emotionally, and favorably, to her freckles. She was in a frame of mind to react favorably because I had intensified her hostility and anger deliberately and then raised in her mind, literally, a vacuum. Because I told her I knew *where* she was when she stole, I knew *what* it was she stole. And I had proof of it. And so, she felt relieved at the accusation of being a thief when it didn't apply. I was really joking with her and it became a fun situation. And she liked her cinnamon rolls or buns or cookies, and I gave her freckles a new name. It was *her* emotions, *her* thinking, *her* reactions that were therapeutic. Although she doesn't know it.

Later, Erickson commented on the story of "Cinnamon Face," "You also ought to learn that it's not what you do, it's not what you say, but what the patient *does, what the* patient *understands."*

I had the opportunity to see a card and note addressed to Dr. Erickson from Cinnamon Face. "Dear Mr. Erickson, I was thinking about you today. I was reading those 'crazy' letters you wrote me. How have you been doing? I will try to remember to send you a valentine. This year I am in sixth grade. You probably don't remember me that well, but if you see my nickname you will. TURN OVER. My name is B—— H—— (Ciniman Face) [sic] Well, I got to by now. By

Cinnimon Face [sic]"

The card was printed in three different shades of purple crayon. And the note was accompanied by a colored photograph of a charming little girl with reddish-brown hair and a face covered with reddish freckles. She was smiling.

PSORIASIS

A young woman said, "I've been trying to screw up my courage for months to come to see you. You notice I have on a high collar and long sleeves and it's summertime. But last night when I saw all the dandruff on the carpet, and this morning all the dandruff in my bed, I thought, "I've got to see a psychiatrist. As long as I have psoriasis, he can't do anything worse to me."

I said, "So you think you've got psoriasis."

She said, "I'd hate to be in the nude. You'd look at my body, at my arms, my neck. I could shed dandruff all over."

I said, "Let me look at the psoriasis. It won't kill me and you won't die."

She showed it to me. I looked at it carefully and I said, "You haven't got more than one-third of the psoriasis that you think you have."

She said, "I came to you for help because you're a doctor. And now you're telling me that I've got less than one-third of all that psoriasis and I can *see* how much I've got, and you downgrade it to a third."

I said, "That's right. You have many *emotions*. You've got a little psoriasis and a lot of emotions. You're alive, you've got emotions; a little psoriasis and a lot of emotions. A lot of emotions on your arms, on your body, and you've called it 'psoriasis.' So you can't have but one-third as much as you think you have."

She said, "How much do I owe you?"

I told her.

She said, "I'll write you a check and I'll never see you again."

Two weeks later she called me and said, "May I have an appointment with you?"

I said, "Yes."

She said, "I want to apologize. I want to see you again."

I said, "There's no need to apologize because I made the right diagnosis and I don't want to be apologized to."

She said, "I guess you're right. I shouldn't apologize. I should be grateful that you made the right diagnosis. I don't have dandruff any more, and look at my arms. Here and there are small patches, but that's all. And the rest of my body too. I stayed mad at you for two weeks."

When Erickson says to the young woman, "You have a little psoriasis and a lot of emotions," he is equating the psoriasis and the emotions, suggesting that the more emotion, the less psoriasis and the more psoriasis, the less emotion. He then gives her the opportunity to direct her emotions toward him. When she got mad at him and stayed mad at him for two weeks, her psoriasis lessened. She had a lot of emotions and a little psoriasis.

Thus Erickson prepares his patients to find a new frame of reference by challenging them, confusing them, or stirring up unpleasant emotions. The reframing is done in harmony with a person's own mental sets and beliefs. In "Whistleberries," he determines first that the patient considers herself religious. With the child in "Cinnamon Face," he adopts a playful attitude that is appropriate when dealing with a child. And he relates to the antagonistic attitude and competitive tendency of the psoriasis patient by challenging her. The psoriasis patient realizes that she was angry. She confirms for herself that Erickson was right and she did have a lot of emotion. On an unconscious level, then, the connection was made that he must be right about the other half of his declaration—that is, she had only one-third of the psoriasis that she thought she had. Her body proceeded to demonstrate this to her by losing most of its rash.

Once "Cinnamon Face" had smiled in relief at hearing herself labeled "Cinnamon Face" instead of a thief, she would be predisposed to smile anytime she thought about her freckles. Thus, her original hatred and anger was replaced by a quietly amused feeling. As Erickson explains, "It became a fun situation." And this fun situation persisted even after she was out of Erickson's presence.

In "Whistleberries," the situation is reframed for the patient from one in which she was humiliated about her loss of control into one in which she could appreciate the exquisite control she actually had—that is, in being able to emit only gas while retaining liquid matter and solid matter in her rectum. She actually was urged to rejoice by dancing in the nude around her apartment while she practiced this control. Of course, on a much more superficial level, Erickson is giving her permission to fart, and this

might have canceled out previous admonitions that this is a terri-
ble thing to do. He is respecting her inhibitions, however, by not
suggesting she do this in public.

Incidentally, Erickson points out that there is an addendum
to the story. This acceptance of her physical being was carried
over to acceptance of other natural functions; thus, she is able to
expose her breast and nurse her baby while talking with him a year
later.

NOT A SINGLE ERECTION

I try to tailor therapy to the individual patient. Now, a doctor
came to me and said, "I had intercourse the first time in a bawdy
house. The experience disgusted me. So much so that in the
twenty years that have gone by I have not had a single erection.
I have hired women at all levels and paid them big money and
told them, 'Make me get an erection.' And they've all failed.

"Now I've found a girl I want to marry. I tried to go to bed
with her. She's very kind and solicitous, but I can't get an erection."

I said, "Let the girl talk to me and it'll be a private talk
between the girl and me and then I'll talk to the two of you
together."

I told the girl, "Go to bed with him every night, but be a
thoroughly cold woman. Don't permit him to touch your breasts,
touch your body in any way at all. Just forbid it. And it's very
important you obey these instructions."

I called the doctor in and said, "I told Mildred that she's to
go to bed with you every night. I told her to reject any attempt
at kissing, touching of her breasts, her genitals, her body. She's
to be totally rejecting of you. And I want that to take place for
three months. Then you come in and discuss the situation with
me."

Early in March he lost control of himself and "raped" her.

Now, Mildred was a very beautiful woman with a beautiful figure. And when he was confronted by the impossibility derived from Mildred, *not from him, it* changed the frame of reference. Mildred *was making intercourse impossible; he wasn't.*

So he didn't have to hang on to his limp penis. Mildred *made it impossible for him.*

Since the patient's first sexual experience in a bawdy house had disgusted him and his attempted self-cures, by "hiring" women, had reinforced his pattern of failure, Erickson determined that his impotence resulted from sex that is easily available. Therefore, Erickson, with the cooperation of the man's girl friend, set up an opposite situation—where sex was forbidden. In his explanation of what happened, Erickson typically uses vague referents. When, in the last sentence, he says, "Mildred made it impossible for him," we (and presumably the patient) wonder what "it" is that is impossible for him: to have intercourse? to hang on to his limp penis, i.e., to masturbate without an erection? to remain impotent? In any case, he managed to transfer the "enemy" outside of the patient. Then, instead of being angry at himself, and subsequently reinforcing his inability to have an erection, the patient could attack the cause of the "impossibility" outside himself, in Mildred. He does this by "raping" her. Once he had had satisfactory sexual relations, with no worry about achieving an erection, he presumably was then able to enjoy making love without such a strong element of aggression.

SLURP, SLURP, SLURP

A fifteen-year-old girl sucked her thumb constantly. Her parents called me up and wept and wailed. They said the girl annoyed them all day long by sucking her thumb. She sucked her thumb on the school bus and the school-bus driver was offended. The other children were, too. The teachers complained about her sucking her thumb. They told her they were going to bring her to me.

The girl came into the office sucking her thumb loudly, defiantly. Her parents were in the other room and could not hear what I was saying to her. "I'm going to tell you that you are very stupid about your thumb sucking," I said.

She said, "You are talking like my parents."

I said, "No, I'm talking intelligently. You are settling for the rather mild discomfort that your parents suffer, the rather mild discomfort that the bus driver suffers. You spread your thumb sucking all around the school. How many thousands of children are there in that school? You spread it to everybody. Now, if you *weren't* stupid, if you were *intelligent,* you'd suck your thumb in a way that would really be a pain in the neck to your father.

"I have found out, from your father and mother, that after dinner, there is an absolutely fixed routine. Your father reads the daily paper. He sits down and he reads it, from cover to cover. I made your parents promise that they would shut their mouths about your thumb sucking. They are not to say a word to you about it.

"So please get a clock. Tonight, after supper, you sit down beside your father and slurp away on your thumb for twenty whole minutes and let your mother, who is a very routine person, get through washing dishes. She likes to do patchwork quilts. After doing the dishes she always sits down and works on her patchwork quilts. After twenty minutes with your father, you sit down beside your mother. Watch the clock and suck your thumb— thoroughly, slurp, slurp, slurp.

"I made your parents both promise that they would not say anything about your thumb sucking. And you can enjoy raising holy hell with their feelings. And they can't do anything about it.

"As for the bus driver—you only see him twice a day. You see the school kids every day. You don't see the school-bus driver or the school kids on Saturday or Sunday. So just spread it around. Now, normally a schoolgirl dislikes some boy or some girl in particular. So *use* your thumb sucking. Every time that student looks at you, pop your thumb into your mouth. And *really* slurp away. And every student dislikes some one teacher. Now, don't spread it uselessly over the other teachers. Every time you see that particular teacher, shove your thumb in your mouth and slurp away."

In less than a month she found that there are *other* things to do. I had made her thumb sucking obligatory and she did not want to be obliged to do anything.

When Erickson points out the "fixed routines" of the parents, he is indirectly drawing the girl's attention to the compulsiveness of her own thumb-sucking behavior. He suggests that she might stop being "stupid" (i.e., acting without awareness or purpose). Instead, she could deliberately express her hostility more effectively. Her thumb-sucking behavior is reframed. No longer is it just a "habit," beyond control. Now it is a useful form of communication—of hostility.

In this story, as in many of Erickson's stories about the treatment of children, he begins with "I sent the parents out of the room and I talked with the child." On one level, he is respecting the child as an individual, away from his parents. On another level, he is talking to the child in all of us. The parents, who often represent coercion, impatience, and lack of acceptance, are banished. They must not interfere with the therapy. On this level, Erickson is telling us to put aside the demands of our own overly stringent superego, our overly strict "shoulds," and allow the potential of the child to emerge and develop. He may be telling us not to bury our childish impulses—our spontaneity, our curios-

*ity, our impetuousness, our explosiveness, and so on—but to chan-
nel these impulses or direct them "intelligently." When, like this
girl, we can see the connection between what we are doing and
the response of others (e.g., their annoyance), we may decide to
stop that particular type of behavior.*

*This type of "symptom prescription" might also be consid-
ered an application of Alfred Adler's dictum about therapy. Adler
once said, "Therapy is like spitting in someone's soup. They can
continue to eat it, but they can't enjoy it." By making the thumb
sucking obligatory, Erickson "spat in this girl's soup."*

7. Learning by Experience

BEING SIX YEARS OLD

I received a letter from my daughter-in-law last week in which she told me about her daughter's sixth birthday. The next day she did something for which her mother reprimanded her, and she told her mother:

"It's awfully hard to be six years old. I've only had one day's experience."

DREAMING

When you go to bed at night you go to bed to sleep, perchance to dream. And in your dream, you do not intellectualize, you experience. I refused to give some candy to my son Lance. I told him that he had already had enough. The next morning he awakened, very happy. He told me, "I ate the whole sack full."

And when I showed him that the sack still contained candy he thought that I must have gone out and bought some more because he *knew* that he had eaten it. And he *had* eaten it—in his dream.

Another time, Bert had teased Lance and Lance wanted me to punish Bert. I refused. The next morning Lance said, "I am glad you gave Bert a licking—but you did not have to use such a *big* baseball bat." He knew I *had* punished Bert severely. He turned his guilt over wishing that his father would punish Bert into criticism of the *severity* of my punishment. So, something had happened to him.

Many subjects who tend to intellectualize, instead of going into a trance, will, some night, when they are thinking about other matters, dream that they are in a trance. And, in that trance state of the dream, they will do certain things. They will come and tell you the next day, "I dreamed a solution to that problem." Therapy is primarily a motivation of the unconscious to make use of all its many and varied learnings.

There are all kinds of experience, and dreaming is one kind of experience. In this story, Erickson is also pointing out that even though the hypnosis may not work, the therapy might. That is, the patient may go home and complete the work in a dream. After having been told this story, an intellectualizing patient may go home and dream that he is in a trance.

SWIMMING

Learning by experience is much more educational than learning consciously. You can learn all the movements of swimming while you're lying on your belly on a piano stool. You can establish your rhythms, breathing, head movement, arm movements, feet movements, and so on. When you get into the water, you only know how to dog-paddle. You have to learn to *swim* in the *water*. And when you have learned that, you have got a learning.

Learning experientially is the most important thing. Now, we have all learned while we are going to school that we should learn consciously. You did things unconsciously, in relationship to the water. And you learned to roll your head, paddle with your hands, and kick with your feet in a certain rhythm—in relationship to the water. And any of you who are not swimmers don't know, can't describe to me, the feeling of your feet in water, the feeling of water on your hands, the suction of the water as you turn your body right and left in the Australian crawl, for example.

When you swim on your back you know about this. How much attention do you pay to the spring of the water under your back as you swim backwards? If you have ever gone skinny-dipping, you will find out what a horrible drag a bathing suit is. The water skips over your skin so much more easily when you are in the nude. And the swimming suit is definitely a handicap.

I am not concerned with how much any of you learn about hypnosis here in this room, because all of you know, from time to time—in that neither-here-nor-there period, when you are not asleep and not awake—you learn a whole lot, in that hypnagogic state, about hypnosis. I used to like to awaken in the morning, have my feet hit the floor as I opened my eyes, and my wife always liked to take fifteen to twenty minutes to wake up slowly, gradually. My blood supply goes instantly to my head. *Her* blood supply goes very slowly. *We all have our own individual patterns.* How many times do you have to go into a trance, maybe a dozen times, until you lose interest in watching the experience yourself?

Have you ever taken a swim in the Great Salt Lake? It looks like water, and feels like water. I knew ahead of time that I couldn't swim in it. I wondered what would happen if I tried to swim. I had all the understanding of the lake being supersaturated salt water. But I had to have the *experience* of trying to swim before I could figure out what would happen to a swimmer who tried to swim. And most hypnotic subjects want to understand *as* they experience. Keep the experience separate. Just let things happen.

Erickson is emphasizing awareness of the body through tactile experience. As he mentions various sensations, rhythms, movements, the listener cannot help remembering similar experiences.

Instead of saying, "Those of you who are swimmers can recall the feeling of your feet in the water . . . ," Erickson puts the statement in the negative and says, "Any of you who are not swimmers can't describe. . . ." Later he makes the suggestion by asking, "How much attention do you pay to the spring of the water under your back as you swim backwards?" He is implying that it is good and worthwhile to focus one's attention on sensory experience.

When Erickson says, "I am not concerned with how much any of you learn about hypnosis here in this room [emphasis mine]," he is offering a long-term posthypnotic suggestion that learning about hypnosis will continue outside of this room. He then elaborates by indirectly suggesting that "this learning" will occur in various special situations such as on awakening. He also suggests that each listener will do "this learning" according to his own "individual patterns." He explains that experiential learning is best done when one is simply experiencing and not examining the experience. He slips in another posthypnotic suggestion— that this will happen after twelve trance experiences. In his later comments, he again emphasizes the importance of not trying to understand experience while it is occurring. This principle applies, of course, to all experiencing, not only to hypnotic experiencing. If one wants to understand experiences it is best that the examining, reviewing, and analyzing be left to a later time, when one has achieved some distance from the experience.

Telling a story such as this one to patients in sex therapy can be very helpful. It would be a good introduction to the description of sensate focus exercises, for example. For patients who are alienated from their sensations, it can be productive to focus on tactile sensations.

TAKE A TASTE

My son Bert could have been an excellent psychiatrist, but he chose farming. He had six boys and one girl. He was concerned about his kids' taking up tobacco, alcohol, drugs, and so on. So, from the very beginning he would show them harmless but interesting-looking stuff, like axle grease. When the kids asked about it, he'd say, "Why don't you take a taste?" Or, he would take a pretty bottle: "Why don't you smell it?" And ammonia isn't pleasant to smell! Every one of the kids learned to be very worried about what they put into their mouths. It was a good way of growing up.

Erickson again expresses his conviction that the best way for people to learn is through experience. The parent, teacher, or therapist provides the opportunity for experience. Bert does not need to provide an actual experience with tobacco, alcohol, or drugs, since he has taught his children, by experience, "to be very worried about what they put into their mouths." He has provided them with experiences, during their formative years, that would lead them to be discriminating. Once they have learned discrimination, they can be trusted to decide for themselves about using tobacco, alcohol, or drugs.

8. Taking Charge of Your Life

ON DEATH AND DYING

[In response to a student who expressed concern that Erickson was dying]

I think that is entirely premature. I have no intention of dying. In fact, that will be the last thing I do!

My mother lived to be ninety-four; my grandmother and great-grandmother were all ninety-three or older. My father died at ninety-seven and a half. My father was planting fruit trees, wondering if he would live long enough to eat any of the fruit. And he was ninety-six or ninety-seven when he was planting fruit trees.

Psychotherapists have a wrong idea about sickness, handicaps, and death. They tend to overemphasize the matter of adjustment to illness, handicaps, and death. There is a lot of hogwash going around about assisting families in grieving. I think you ought to bear in mind that the day you are born is the day you start dying. And some are more efficient than others and don't waste a lot of time dying, and there are others who wait a long time.

My father had a massive coronary attack at eighty. He was unconscious when he was taken to the hospital. My sister went with him; the doctor told my sister, "Now, don't have too much hope. Your father is an old man. He worked hard all of his life and he's had a very, very severe coronary."

And my sister said, "I snorted at the doctor and said, 'You don't know my dad!' "

When my father recovered consciousness the doctor was there. My father said, "What happened?"

The doctor told him, "Don't worry, Mr. Erickson, you've had a very bad coronary attack, but in two or three months you'll be home as good as new."

My father, outraged, said, "Two or three months, my foot! What you mean is I've got to waste a whole week!" He was home in a week's time.

He was eighty-five when he had his second and similar heart attack. The same doctor was there. My father recovered consciousness and said, "What happened?"

The doctor said, "Same thing."

My father groaned and said, "Another week wasted."

He had a drastic abdominal operation and had nine feet of intestine removed. When he came out of anesthesia, in recovery, he asked the nurse, "Now what happened?"

She told him and he groaned and said, "Instead of a whole week it'll be ten days."

His third heart attack occurred when he was eighty-nine. He recovered consciousness and said, "Same thing, doctor?"

The doctor said, "Yes."

My father said, "Now this is getting to be a bad habit of wasting a week at a time."

He had his fourth coronary at ninety-three. When he recovered consciousness he said, "Honest, Doc, I thought the fourth would carry me off. Now I'm beginning to lose faith in the fifth."

At ninety-seven and a half he and two of my sisters were planning a weekend trip to the old farming community. All his peers were dead and some of their children. They planned whom to visit, what motel to stay in, what restaurants to eat at. Then they walked out to the car. When they reached the car my father said, "Oh, I forgot my hat."

He ran back for his hat. My sisters waited a reasonable length of time and then looked at each other coolly and said, "This is it."

They went in. Dad was dead on the floor of a massive cerebral hemorrhage.

My mother fell and broke her hip at ninety-three. She said, "This is a ridiculous thing for a woman my age to do. I'll get over it." And she did.

When she fell and broke the other hip a year later, she said, "Getting over that first broken hip took a lot out of me. I don't think I'll get over this one, but nobody will ever say I didn't try."

I knew, and the rest of the family knew, by my blank face, that the second broken hip would be her death. She died of congestive pneumonia, the "old woman's friend."

My mother's favorite quotation was "Into each life some rain must fall. Some days must be dark and dreary." Longfellow's poem "The Rainy Day."

My father and my mother enjoyed life thoroughly, always. I try to impress upon patients: "Enjoy life and enjoy it thoroughly." And the more humor you can put into life, the better off you are.

I don't know where that student got the idea I'm going to die. I'm going to put that off.

Erickson wanted death to be something that was not anxiety provoking, and emphasized that life was for the living. His father, he tells us, was planting fruit trees at the age of ninety-seven. The orientation was to the future. His father was active and he died while going to do something—he wanted to get his hat and to visit people. Jeffrey Zeig believes that the comment "Oh, I forgot my hat" came from an unconscious recognition that something was going on inside his head.

Erickson often followed this story by saying that his father was right to lose faith in the fourth coronary. His father died at the age of ninety-seven and one-half, of a cerebral hemorrhage. Erick-

son also shared his father's attitude toward illness, which is that
it is "part of the roughage of life." Every diet needs some rough-
age, and Erickson would point out that soldiers on K-rations know
how important roughage is in the diet. Tragedies, deaths, illness
are all part of the roughage in life.

In his last years, Erickson spent considerable time preparing
people for his death. He did not want extended grieving, and he
used jokes and quips to diffuse people's anxiety. Once he mis-
quoted Tennyson by saying, "Let there be no moaning at the bar
when my ship sets out to sea." He talked openly about death.
And, like his father, he was oriented toward the future when he
died. He was looking forward to teaching on the following Mon-
day. Typically, there was no funeral or burial. His ashes were
scattered on Squaw Peak.

Erickson's final comment on the story: "I don't know where
that student got the idea that I am going to die. I am going to
put that off." Put what off? Dying? Or the student's idea?

I WANT A PAIR

When my father ran away from home at sixteen he pinned
a note to his pillow, walked into the depot, plunked down the
nickels and dimes he'd saved, and said, "Give me a ticket for as
far as that will go." He landed in Beaver Dam, Wisconsin, a
country village. He walked down the street and looked at the local
farmers, some of whom drove horses and some of whom had
oxcarts. Then he stepped up to a silver-haired man driving an
oxcart and he said, "Don't you want a bright young man to help
on your farm?"

The boy said his name was Charlie Roberts. He said he had no
family, no money, nothing, and finally the silver-haired farmer
said, "Hop in the cart. You can come with me and work on the farm."

On the way home, the farmer stopped his oxcart and said, "You stay in that cart. I've got to see my son-in-law." A girl in a flowered dress peeked out from behind a maple tree and Charlie said, "Whose girl are you?" She said quietly, "I'm my poppa's." He said, "You're mine, now."

When my father made a formal proposal seven years later, my mother reached in her little pocket and handed him a miniature mitten, because in that rural community a refusal of a proposal was called "giving a man the mitten." My father stalked out of the house. He couldn't sleep all night long and the next morning he walked in on my mother and said, "I didn't ask you for a mitten, I want a pair." The mitten was knitted from wool that my mother had washed, carded, and spun into yarn.

She had knitted that mitten when she was aged seventeen, and the proposal occurred when she was twenty. My father knew my mother. My mother knew my father. And I taught school in that country school where my mother went to school.

The name "Charlie Roberts" was adopted by Erickson's father when he left home at the age of sixteen. The stories that Erickson told about his father highlight the father's sense of adventure, his confidence and ability to get his own way. The latter trait recurs in all of the stories that Erickson told about his family.

The message here appears to be that you can set your eyes on a goal, stick with it, and not accept "no" for an answer. Of course, you must also do what is necessary to achieve that goal. Erickson glides over the fact that Charlie Roberts worked for his future father-in-law for several years. In other stories, rewards do not simply come because you are stubborn and persistent. The correct strategy must be applied and you must work in a way that is valued by the society you want to impress.

Even so, as Erickson points out in the next story, you can't win them all.

DISAGREEMENTS

When we were first married my bride asked my mother, "When Dad and you disagree, what happens?"

Mother said, "I speak my mind freely, then I shut up."

Then she went out into the yard and asked my father, "What did you do when you and Mother disagreed?"

And my father said, "I said what I had to say and then I shut up."

Betty said, "Well, what happened then?"

My father said, "One or the other of us had their way. It always worked out that way."

Erickson's parents were married for almost seventy-five years. Obviously their marital harmony was achieved on the basis of mutual respect, and they applied the principle of never trying to force an opinion.

WORKING HER WAY THROUGH COLLEGE

Kristi said to me, "You worked your way through medical school. Of course, you were crippled, that made it hard. I'm younger than you were then, and I'm going to work my way through college."

I said, "Okay, kid."

"Now, the next question is, how much board and room are you going to charge me?"

That was a serious question. "The average board and room is

twenty-five dollars a week, but you won't have the privileges of washing dirty dishes, vacuuming the floor, making the beds, using the telephone, raiding the refrigerator."

She said, "That's an easy ten dollars. Well, I've got to go downtown and find a job."

"Do you want a reference?"

She said, "My social-security number and my high-school diploma are my references."

For about eight months we didn't know where she worked. She went down to Good Samaritan Hospital, said she would like a job typing in the records room, and they looked at that little ninety-eight-pound girl, and explained to her, "You have to know a lot of medical terms, physiological terms, psychiatric terms."

She said, "Yes, I know. That's why I went to the library and read Dorland's Medical Dictionary *and Stedman's* Medical Dictionary *and Warren's* Psychological Dictionary."

So they tried her out and kept her.

At the end of a year, there was a lot of teenage rebellion in her and she decided to go to Michigan. Her brother asked her if she wanted any money and she said, "No." Mother asked her, and so did I. We all got the answer "No."

So she packed up her Phoenix winter wardrobe, took the train in late January to Michigan, and it was eleven below zero when she arrived. It took her three days to enroll and get a job in the dean's office. The dean looked at her class cards and saw that she had signed up for nineteen hours. Working students were only allowed to take sixteen hours. Kristi said, "Well, I'm working in your office and you'll have the opportunity to keep your eye on my work and on my grades and you'll know what to do." He said, "That's right, I will."

So she took nineteen hours. But she didn't tell the dean one thing. The job in his office was all-important. That's where the dormitory cards for coeds were kept.

She had located an elderly couple with a married son and a married daughter and persuaded them that young life in the home is desirable. Once a week, the married son took grandpa and grandma out to dinner. And once a week the daughter took grandpa and grandma out to dinner. Kristi sold them a bill of goods and she did a lot of cooking and cleaning and got free room and board, and the married son and the married daughter paid her baby-sitting fees.

Why was it important that she work in the dean's office, where the cards were kept? So that the fact that she was not living in the dormitory would not be discovered. She never told anybody except us and a few trusted friends about her job in a bargain-basement store.

Erickson often used stories about the resourcefulness of his children to encourage patients to utilize their own resources. "Authority" is utilized to achieve the desired goals—in this case being able to take nineteen hours and to live off-campus. Once again, authorities (and, symbolically, "inner authority") are seen as allies rather than opponents.

PEARSON'S BRICK

Robert Pearson, a psychiatrist in Michigan, had a family practice. He was the only doctor within sixty miles. The nearest hospital was sixty miles away. He had sent his family out to visit relatives because he had a builder tear down a chimney on the third story of his house. The builder didn't know that Pearson was home, and he was tearing down bricks and throwing them on the ground. Bob carelessly walked out of the house as a brick was falling. It hit him on the forehead and fractured his skull.

Bob started to sink to his knees, then caught himself and said,

"If only Erickson was here. But, damn it, he's in Arizona. I'd better take charge myself." So he quickly produced a local anesthesia. He drove sixty miles to the hospital, went through the admissions procedure. Then he called a neurosurgeon and he told the neurosurgeon, "I won't need an anesthetic." And the neurosurgeon politely insisted on his having an anesthesia. So Bob told the anesthesiologist, "Keep a written record of everything said while I'm under the anesthesia."

After the operation Bob recovered consciousness promptly and he told the anesthesiologist, "The surgeon said this, said this, said this." He had total recall of everything that had been said, and the surgeon was horrified to find out Bob had heard him discussing whether they should put in a silver plate or not.

Then Bob told the surgeon, "Next Wednesday [this was on a Thursday] I've got to be in San Francisco delivering a paper at the annual convention."

The surgeon said, "You'll be lucky if you're in bedroom slippers and a bathrobe in a month's time."

And Bob said, "I'd like to reach an understanding with you. On Tuesday, you come in and give me a complete physical examination. If you find nothing wrong, I go to San Francisco. If you find something wrong, I'll stay in the hospital." Bob said that surgeon really sweated blood during the physical examination and reluctantly discharged him.

In San Francisco I saw Bob with a Band-Aid on his forehead. He slipped off the Band-Aid and said, "What do you think about that?"

I said, "How did you get scratched?" It was a hairline scar.

Bob said, "I had a skull fracture," and he told me the story.

This story, like Erickson's story about his father's heart attacks, demonstrates the power of mind over body in overcoming serious physical traumas. Pearson says, "I better take charge my-

self." This idea applies to all of us, and "taking charge" can occur in extreme danger, when, out of dire necessity, we discover inner resources we did not know we possessed.

Pearson's story demonstrates the fact that we generally have more knowledge of what is going on than we allow ourselves to know. He is able to recall even things that are said when he is under anesthesia. It is interesting that he was not only able to do this but able to anticipate doing this, since he had asked the anesthesiologist in advance to "keep a written record of everything said while I am under the anesthesia." Of course, when Pearson gives others tasks such as this, he is taking charge of the situation, even in this particular situation where all of us would be most passive and helpless—under anesthesia.

One theme of this story is that the usual roles that we assume are reversed. The patient takes charge while the surgeons and anesthesiologist serve him. In actuality this is the doctors' function. But most patients regress when they become sick; they put the doctor in the position of the omnipotent, powerful parent. The doctor's actual function is to use his knowledge to treat and cure in accordance with the wishes and needs of the patient.

CALLUSES

A construction worker fell forty stories and wound up paralyzed except for the use of his arms. That was permanent. That was for life. He wanted to know what to do about his painful situation. I said, "There isn't much you can really do. You can develop calluses on your pain nerves. That way you won't feel the pain so much.

"Now, life will prove very boring, so have your friends bring you cartoons, comic books, and the nurse will furnish you with paste and scissors. You make scrapbooks of cartoons, jokes, and funny sayings. You can really amuse yourself thoroughly making those scrapbooks. Every time one of your fellow workmen lands in the hospital, send him a scrapbook."

So he made I don't know how many hundreds of scrapbooks.

At first Erickson redirects the patient's concern from pain to calluses—something that the patient, a construction worker, knew about. Then he needs to direct him to something that would involve him in life, in living. He cites the truism that life will prove very boring. He directs the patient to become involved in a social activity—first having friends bring him cartoons and comic books and then giving back to others the scrapbooks that he will make. So the fellow became involved in an activity, without realizing that it would also keep him involved with people. He became more self-sufficient and able to live "outside of" his pain.

9. Capturing the Innocent Eye

When we think of seeing things with a fresh eye, as if for the first time, we are reminded of some popular meditation techniques. In The Book of Secrets, *Bhagwan Shree Rajneesh* describes a sutra in which the technique is: *"See as if for the first time a beauteous person or an ordinary object."* He points out that we get into the habit of not seeing familiar objects, friends, or family. *"They say nothing is new under the sky. Really, nothing is old under the sky. Only the eyes become old, accustomed to things; then nothing is new. For children everything is new: that is why everything gives them excitement . . ."* He ends the chapter with *"Look freshly, as if for the first time . . . This will give you a freshness to your look. Your eyes will become innocent. Those innocent eyes can see. Those innocent eyes can enter into the inner world."*

We have already seen this approach of "looking freshly" in several of Erickson's tales. In "Training the U.S. Rifle Team to Beat the Russians" (p. 107), Erickson instructs the riflemen to think of each shot as if it were the first shot. In "Walking on Glare Ice" (p. 110), the subject is led to put aside previous associations, since his eyes are closed and he is not aware that he is walking on ice. Subsequently he does not walk stiffly, preparing to fall. He can approach each step "innocently," responding appropriately to his kinesthetic sense and trusting his sense of balance. In fact, the value of focusing on the present moment is repeatedly empha-sized in the tales. The reader is likely to think of a tale, such as "Walking Down the Street" (p. 69), while actually walking down *the street. When this happens, he is bound to look at whatever he is doing with a fresh eye.*

Looking with a clear view, with "openness," is emphasized both in this chapter and in the one that follows, "Observe: Notice Distinctions." The main difference is that the stories in the latter illustrate an "educated" clear vision that utilizes experience to interpret data.

THINKING LIKE CHILDREN

How can we learn to think like children again and regain some creativity?

Watch little children. My youngest daughter went through college in three years, got a master's in her fourth year of college, and completed medical school in two years and nine months. When she was very young she would draw pictures and she'd remark as she was drawing: "Drawing this picture is hard. I hope I get it done so I'll know what I'm drawing."

Watch little children drawing pictures. "Is this a barn? No, it's a cow. No, it's a tree." The picture is whatever they want it to be.

Most little children have good eidetic imagery, and some have imaginary playmates. They can have a tea party that they can change into a game in the orchard. Then they change that tea party in the orchard into a hunt for Easter eggs. Children are very ignorant, so they've got lots of room to change things around.

In a trance state, you've got billions of brain cells at your service that ordinarily you don't use. And children are very honest. "I don't like you." Whereas you would say, "Pleased to meet you."

You follow a very careful routine socially without realizing you are restricting your behavior. In hypnotic trance, you are free.

GHOST ROGER

We had a dog, a male basset named Roger. When he died, my wife was very tearful. The next day in the mail there was a letter to her from Ghost Roger, from the great bone yard up yonder.

Of course Ghost Roger was quite prolific as a letter writer. And Ghost Roger picked up a lot of gossip from other ghosts, about how the kids behaved when they were young. My grandchildren read those letters and have inside information on their parents.

Children play with words and they play with ideas. And with their eidetic imagery they have cats and dogs all around them, except grown-ups can't see them.

When we were driving from Michigan to Wisconsin to visit my parents, I could look ahead to see what was coming up. I used to talk about eating pancakes: "How big a stack would you like to eat?"

We'd come alongside a haystack: "There's a nice stack to eat." A stack of pancakes, a stack of hay. And so we learned to play a lot of games that way.

In hypnosis I think the best thing to do is to make use of whatever you can. It might pertain to a person's childhood.

WHY DO YOU CARRY THAT CANE?

I gave a lecture to a large medical group, and when it was over, one of the doctors said, "I enjoyed your lecture and I followed your blackboard drawings, your illustrations, and explanations. Now, there is one thing I can't understand. Why didn't you use the poker that was lying in the trough? Why do you carry around the cane that you use for a poker?"

I said, "I carry around a cane because I limp. It is also handy as a poker."

He said, "You don't limp."

And he learned that a lot of other members of the audience had not noticed that I limped. They just thought that it was an affectation, that I carried my cane in my pocket and then used it as a poker.

I have walked into many homes and a small child has said right away, "What's wrong with your leg?" Because they notice that. A child's mind is a rather open thing. Adults tend to restrict themselves. Every magician will tell you, "Don't let children too near or they will see through the trick." Adults have closed minds. They think they are watching everything. They aren't watching. They have got a routine way of looking.

MAGIC SHOWS

I had a magician put on a show for my children. He made the children stay as far away as possible. He gave me leave to be close. He showed me a rabbit in a pasteboard box in another room and I watched him carefully. There were only his two hands to watch. That was not difficult. And when he left that room I knew he had not taken the rabbit with him. Later on in the show he produced a hat and he took the rabbit out. Now, I had carefully watched to be sure that his hands did not open that pasteboard box to take out the rabbit. The show went on for about a half an hour when the rabbit suddenly appeared in his hat. I found out later he had distracted my attention for just a moment and had taken the rabbit out of the pasteboard box and had slipped it into a pocket in his gown. I never saw the rabbit wriggling around in the gown. He took the hat out for me to see and there was a rabbit in it.

One of my kids, sitting on the far side of the room, said, "You took that out of your gown!"

10. *Observe: Notice Distinctions*

In this chapter Erickson not only points out the importance of observing and of noticing distinctions; he also he gives several examples of setting up situations so that he will have phenomena to observe, from which he can obtain important information. In other words, if the patient himself does not manifest helpful or informative behavior (as does the patient in "The Right Psychiatrist"), Erickson sets up a situation that encourages such behavior. Commonly, we refer to situations that we set up as "tests." Erickson does this in actuality in testing a two-year-old child for deafness. In a less direct way, in the case I've called "Sneezing," he introduces a test question that leads to important information.

In the following stories observing is linked with judgment and experience.

THE RIGHT PSYCHIATRIST

When you listen to people talk, listen to all the possibilities. Be comprehensive and unrestrictive in your thinking and don't just try to apply the third line, the fourth page of Carl Rogers's book, to *any* patient. Think comprehensively.

A certain beautiful young woman came into my office, sat down, picked some lint off her sleeve, and said, "I know I don't have an appointment with you, Dr. Erickson. I've been to Baltimore and I've seen all of your friends there. I've been to New York and seen your friends there; I've been to Boston and Detroit and none of them were the right psychiatrist for me. I've come to Phoenix to see if you are the right psychiatrist for me."

I said, "That shouldn't take long." I took down her name, age, address, a telephone number, and asked a few other questions and said, "Madam, I am the right psychiatrist for you."

"Aren't you a bit conceited, Dr. Erickson?"

I said, "No, I'm just stating a fact. I am the right psychiatrist for you."

She said, "That sounds awfully conceited."

I said, "It isn't a matter of conceit. It's a matter of fact—and, if you want me to prove it, I can prove it—by asking you a simple question. Now, think it over carefully, because I don't think you want me to ask that question."

She said, "No, but go ahead and ask your question."

I said, "How long have you been wearing women's clothes?"

And he said, "How did you know?"

I *was* the right psychiatrist. Now, how did I know? That's right. By the way he picked the lint off his sleeve. As a man I never "detour." I don't have anything to detour around. And women do have. He brushed the lint off without detouring. Only a man does that. And girls learn to do it even before you can see signs of changes in their breasts. In watching my daughters I discovered that happened somewhere around ten years of age. When, for example, Betty Alice was about ten years old and had to pick something off the bookcase or radio, she lifted her arm *this* way (as if to avoid a large breast). I told Mrs. Erickson, "When Betty Alice takes her bath have a look at her breasts." Mrs. Erickson came out and said, "There's just the beginning of a change in her nipples."

A tomboy runs like a boy, throws a ball like a boy. Suddenly one day she runs like a girl, throws a ball like a girl. She runs like a boy because her pelvis is boys' size. And one day it gets a millimeter over a boy's size and she starts being a girl in her running.

Boys go through a stage where they are always looking in a mirror. They have a good reason. When they feel their face, the fact is that the skin of their face is becoming thicker. Thick enough, in fact, to grow whiskers. It has to get thicker before it can grow whiskers. And the thicker skin feels differently. And the boy notices something different about his face. What in hell is it? And his sisters call him vain because he is always looking in the mirror!

HOW WOULD YOU TEST
A TWO-YEAR-OLD?

When I examined the state-orphanage children, I had to sort out the children who could not see very well, had defects of hearing, learning disabilities. And how would you test a one- or two-year-old for hearing? How would you test a two-year-old who was totally deaf? How would you discover that? And you were a total stranger. The child had never seen you.

The attendants at the orphanage thought I was not really in my right mind. I had them bring in the child walking backwards, with the attendant who led him in also walking backwards. And I had a tin pan on the side behind the desk. I dropped it on the floor. That was a heavy paperweight. And the attendant looked around and the *deaf child looked at the floor*. He felt quivers in the floor. Now, if *I* could think of that, why couldn't you? When you want to find things out about your patients, observe. Observe their behavior.

PABLUM

When a six-month-old baby who is being fed Pablum looks at its mother's face and the mother is thinking, "That horrible stuff —it just stinks," the baby reads the headlines on mother's face and spits it out.

All you have to do is watch small children study mother's face or father's face. They know just when to stop short of receiving a rebuke. And know just how many times to ask for candy and get it. No matter how many "nos" they receive. They can hear the weakening of the "no." They know when the "no" is very weak, and an urgent request for candy yields a "yes."

Erickson is saying that when you were a small child you were aware of the tone and other metamessages that accompanied words. He is reminding us that we were influenced by our parents' attitudes and tastes at a time when we were in no position to test them for ourselves. This type of influence is instrumental not only in determining our habits, values, and tastes, but also, unfortunately, in our adoption of parents' fears, prejudices, and phobias.

When he told this story to therapists, I believe he was also saying to them, "Why don't you really pay attention to these extraverbal messages, now?" Incidentally, his repeated use of the words "know" and "no" was characteristic. He may be suggesting to a patient that he can "know" that he can say "no" to a symptom, for example. He ends the story on an "up" note, with a "yes." The indirect or covert message, finally, is that the "no," the negatives, will become weaker and weaker and the patient will be left with a positive attainment of success or relief—with a "yes."

HOW MANY DIFFERENT WAYS?

There was a university student who had been captain of the baseball team in high school and he had been captain of the football team in high school. He wanted to enter A.S.U. [Arizona State University]. But he was found to have a normal one-inch difference in the length of his forearms. He was distraught. He came to me and said, "You don't understand what it is to be crippled."

He couldn't study, he couldn't work, he couldn't go into sports. That short forearm crippled him. Doctors told his mother the facts and said that he was preschizoid.

Now, when a patient tells me that I don't understand pain and that I don't understand being crippled I assume they are wrong. I do. But I can point out very clearly that being paralyzed after graduating from high school hasn't interfered with me at all. And I couldn't move any part of my body except my eyeballs. I learned body language.

And when I went to college, the first year I saw Frank Bacon in *Lightning*. He became a star, saying the word "no" in the course of the play with sixteen different meanings. I went back again the next night and I counted the different meanings.

Erickson may be pointing out the difference between useful noting of differences and obsessive or hypochondriacal focusing on minimal differences, such as on a normal difference between the length of one's forearms.

A DIFFERENT SHADE OF GREEN

I sent one of my patients, who is a heroin addict, to sit on the lawn until he made a fantastic discovery! He was an allergist and his perception of color was phenomenal. After about an hour and a half of sitting on the lawn, he came dashing into the house and said, *"Do you realize that every blade of grass is a different shade of green?"* And he arranged them from very light to very dark. He was so surprised! The amount of chlorophyll in each leaf differs. Chlorophyll differs according to the rainy season, to the fertility of the soil.

Another time I had him sit on the lawn facing east. He came in and said, "The cypress tree in the next lot is leaning toward the sun, leaning southward. I turned and looked and found that you have five cypress trees on your lawn and they are all leaning southward."

I told him, "I discovered that on my first trip to Phoenix, going all around the city, checking up on that. The first time I saw a heliotropic tree it amazed me. You usually think of trees growing straight up. And a heliotropic tree! By the sunflower you can tell the time of day."

Have you ever heard of a flower-bed clock? My grandmother had a flower-bed clock. Morning glories opened in the morning, certain other flowers opened at seven o'clock, others at eight, others at nine, others at ten, others at noon. And there were the evening primroses, for example. The night-blooming cereus opens at about ten-thirty or eleven o'clock at night.

The allergist, trained to distinguish different skin colorations, obviously had also developed a generalized ability to perceive fine distinctions in shade and color. Of course, while purportedly talking about observing natural phenomena, Erickson is interspersing suggestions about "opening." His comments serve as posthypnotic suggestions, so that every time the listener looks at heliotropic trees or at evening primroses he will have associations about "opening." Subsequently he is likely to react with an opening up, not only of perceptions, but also of emotions.

ABROAD

A new patient was already seated when I arrived. I took her name and address and so on, and I asked why she wanted to see me.

She said, "I have a phobia—about airplanes."

I said, "Madam, you were sitting in that chair when I arrived in the office. Will you please walk out to the waiting room and return and sit down." She didn't like this, but she did so. And I said, "Now, for your problem?"

"My husband is taking me a-broad in September and I have a deathly fear of being on an airplane."

I said, "Madam, when a patient comes to a psychiatrist there can be no withholding of information. I know something about you. I am going to ask you an unpleasant question. Because patients can't be helped if they are withholding information. Even if it seems to be unrelated."

She said, "All right."

And I said, "Does your husband know about your love affair?"

She said, "No, but how did you?"

I said, "Your body language told me."

Her ankles were crossed. I can't do it. Her right leg was crossed over the left one and the foot tucked around the ankle. She was completely locked up. In my experience, every married woman who is having an affair who does not want it known always locks herself up that way.

She said, "A-broad," not abroad—one word. She paused between "a" and "broad." She brought her lover in to see me. They had been dating for a number of years. Then she came in to see me about breaking up with him. Her lover came to me because he had a horrible headache, daily. He had some marital problems with *his* wife and the kids, so I asked to see his wife. I told him

I would want to see the children. The wife came in and locked herself up. I said to her, "So you're having an affair."

She said, "Yes, did my husband tell you?"

I said, "No, I got it from your body language. Now I know why your husband has a headache."

She said, "He suggested that I have an affair—some years ago. I found it very pleasant. Then he discovered he didn't want me to continue. I'm not sure that he suspects I am continuing, but there are times when I think he knows I am."

Then I asked her husband while he was in a trance about his advising his wife to have an affair. He said, "I was pretty busy at the time and didn't think I was discharging my husbandly duties. Soon I began to feel jealous and asked her to stop. She said she would, but I keep noticing evidence that says she is continuing the affair—only I don't want to know that she is."

I said, "That's your headache. What do you want to do about it?"

He said, "I'll have my headache."

At one time he was the head of the Democratic party in Arizona. He gave up those duties to give more attention to his wife—but it was too late then.

Some people keep pain because they don't want to know something. So they won't think about something.

Erickson observes that the patient says the words "a-broad" in a peculiar way. Apparently she is calling herself a "broad" because of her unfaithfulness. He also distinguishes visually that she sits in a particular way.

As with almost all of his tales, Erickson used this one for multiple purposes. At the end, he makes a very important point —that people have the right to choose to keep a symptom if losing the symptom might involve greater pain and discomfort. In this case, the hurt to the husband's pride would be more painful to

*him than his headache. When he gave up his position as "head"
of the Democratic party to reestablish himself as "head" of his
family, it was too late. The pain in his head may symbolically
represent the awareness, on some level, that he had been "decapi-
tated." And the pain also serves to prevent him from facing his
situation. If he were to own up to knowing that his wife was
unfaithful, he either would feel called upon to separate from her
or he would feel impotent and ineffectual. He chooses to keep the
headache.*

SNEEZING

A woman told me, "I've seen twenty-six doctors for a physical
examination. One of them put me in the hospital for two weeks
to run tests on me. Another one kept me in the hospital for a week
and ran tests on me. Finally, they told me, 'You'd better see a
psychiatrist, you're rather slaphappy about having physical examinations.' "

The woman told me that story. I asked her, "What unusual
thing did you do during each physical examination that interrupted the doctor's examination?" She thought a long time before
answering, "Well, I always sneezed when they started to examine
my right breast."

I said, "Your age is forty-eight and you always sneeze when
they touch your right breast. You told those doctors you had a
youthful history of gonorrhea and syphilis and you sneeze when
your right breast is touched and they always interrupt their examination of the breast."

She said, "That's right."

I said, "Well, I'm going to send you to a gynecologist and you
can listen to what I tell him over the phone."

I called up the gynecologist and said, "I have a forty-eight-
year-old woman in my office. I think she's got a lump in her right

breast. I don't know whether it's benign or malignant. There are certain psychological indications. Now, I'm sending the woman to your office, and I want you to give her a thorough examination of that right breast. And, if there's anything wrong, send her to the hospital directly from your office or she'll be one of those patients who runs away."

And he examined her right breast. He took her to the hospital immediately. He operated on her for a malignancy of the breast.

Patients give away the fears that they are trying to hide. Here Erickson is telling therapists to observe not only what we can see, but to look for the things that a patient is trying to hide. As he points out, patients often reveal these things indirectly, by trying to draw attention away from them.

He pointed out to the patient that she was not reticent in talking about her history of venereal disease, yet she drew attention away from her right breast. The implication is that she was terrified of learning that she had breast cancer. Indeed, Erickson feared that her fear of facing her diagnosis (one that she had already made for herself) might also cause her to avoid surgery.

MAGIC, THE SUPERNATURAL, AND ESP

Like Houdini, Erickson dismissed so-called supernatural and ESP experiences as being based on trickery, illusion, or highly developed observational powers. His attitude was summarized in a letter to Dr. Ernest F. Pecci, dated June 8, 1979, in which he wrote:

"I feel that I should inform you that I do not believe that the field of parapsychology is scientifically established and I also feel that the so-called evidence for the existence of these faculties is based on false mathematical logic, misinterpretation of data, over-

looking of minimal sensory cues, biased interpretation, and, fre-quently, on outright fraud. I have worked for over fifty years to disassociate the study of hypnosis from mystical and unscientific connotations."

In the stories that follow, Erickson gives some entertaining examples of his own ability to fool fortune-tellers, knowing that they have learned to observe and interpret minimal body move-ments, including those of the lips, neck (around the vocal chords), and face. He then reveals a method that he used to "magically" locate hidden objects. Then he tells a story, which he loved to repeat, about how he fooled J. B. Rhine into believing that he possessed tremendous powers of ESP. In all these situations, Erickson is careful to point out that one need not resort to "super-natural" explanations. Most of the "ESP" feats that he describes can be explained by perfectly "normal" means. The communica-tions are made by the sense of sight and touch. In each situation the "magician" has simply trained himself to observe the "mini-mal sensory cues" that most of us ignore.

FORTUNE-TELLERS

Any simple explanation that absolves you from doing any thinking is readily accepted. I'll tell you one experience of mine. A good hypnotic subject of mine went to a fortune-teller. That fortune-teller told him intimate details about his family. And Harold was tremendously impressed. Without Harold's knowl-edge—and Harold knew my family very well—I wrote out a false name for my father, my mother, for my eight siblings, and the wrong birthplace for them. I gave many false details. I put all this into an envelope and had Harold put it into his inside jacket pocket.

Then I went with Harold to the fortune-teller. To Harold's

astonishment, the fortune-teller told me my father's name was Peter, my mother's name was Beatrice, and he gave all the false names and false places; he gave all the false knowledge. He did not pay any attention to Harold and I suppose he thought Harold's expression of bewilderment meant that he was impressed. And he gave all that false information and then we left.

Harold said to me, "Your father's name is Albert. How could you say Peter?"

I said, "I kept thinking 'Peter, Peter, Peter' and 'Beatrice, Beatrice, Beatrice.' "

So Harold ceased to have a belief in the fortune-teller.

In New Orleans a fortune-teller came and told a doctor friend and his girl friend's fortunes correctly. And then he told my wife, Betty, that eventually she would fall in love with me. He told her the names that we would pick out for our children. Betty and I, when we saw the fortune-teller coming, had agreed that we would give him all the data he wanted. This would make a big impression on my friend and his girl friend. We gave the data to the fortune-teller by subliminal speech. Haven't you watched people count and move their lips as they count? Or watch people read and move their lips? Now, my lips are really so stiff and swollen inside that I can't really do it so that I can confuse a fortune-teller.

In both of the situations described above, the fortune-teller was able to "mind read" by deciphering subliminal or subvocal speech. Erickson had also developed this skill and this may have contributed to his reputation as a mind reader and magician.

MIND READING

At Cornell they were making a big fuss about an idiot savant who would multiply six-digit figures. He could give you the square root, the cube root, of six- and eight-place figures almost instantly. And he had one other trick. He would tell someone to hide a pin anywhere in the building. Then he would walk around with hand contact and he would read that person's mind, he said.

When they were discussing this at Cornell I suggested, "Why don't you hide a pin in some building? You don't need to tell me whether you did it on the second floor, on the first floor, or where, but we'll hold hands and walk around the campus and I'll find the pin."

I found the pin on the second floor, stuck in the frame of a painting. All you do is hold hands, you walk along, and the person withdraws slightly when you get near the pin. So as soon as I found a minimal withdrawal as I approached certain steps, of course I went upstairs. When you reach the top of the stairs there is tension again. Which way to turn? You turn one way and the hands relax. You turn the other way and they tense. So you go around in a circle!

MAGIC TRICKS

I learned some simple magic tricks when I was an intern and then a special resident in psychiatry at Colorado Psychopathic Hospital. They had just started a delinquent-boys child-guidance clinic and each member of the psychopathic hospital had to go down there and the boys resented it terribly. Each staff man served two weeks and all dreaded this. It was torture, because the boys were so antagonistic. When it came my turn, and the boy entered, glaring at me, I engaged in a simple magic trick. I turned away from him so that he couldn't see my trick. He promptly showed me that he could get around that and he demanded that I show him the trick. Then I had to do another one. We ended up the best of friends. So I learned half a dozen tricks and the word got around and the boys all wanted to see me. They wanted something from me, and, thus, I *got* what I wanted from them. It was a simple matter of getting them to play with you without their realizing that you are playing *them.*

"It was a simple matter of getting them to play with you without their realizing that you are playing them." This state-ment summarizes one of Erickson's most important principles— that of engaging the patient's interest while the therapist, often by the use of subliminal suggestions, "plays" the patient's uncon-scious mind. That is, the therapist evokes "music" from the patient in the form of past learnings and knowledge that have been previously inaccessible to the patient. At first, most patients must experience themselves as instruments and allow the thera-pist to play them. With experience they can then learn to play themselves.

ESP WITH J. B. RHINE

Rhine was at a table with some subjects, demonstrating ESP. At another table, some others and I were very distrustful of Rhine. We squeezed down in our seats so that we could get a slanting view of the cards. It was night and there were electric lamps on the table. The cards were lying on the table and Rhine would turn one over. We got our heads down and got a slanting light from the card. And we could see the star impression, the diamond impression, as it showed through on the card. You see, the original cards were stamp impressed. That slight impression on the back of the card reflected light differently and if you got down at the right angle you could see it. You look at something and you see it smooth and you turn it and you can see that glimmer of roughness. So Gilbert, Watson [the others at the table], and I volunteered as subjects—and Rhine thought he had three perfect subjects, because we all read him all twenty-five cards perfectly.

As Erickson is illustrating, it is not necessary to be a trained observer to notice such distinctions as the impression on the backs of the cards. In some cases it is only necessary to look at things from a different angle or perspective.

In the following story he tells of a young man who combined careful observation with a highly developed memory to perform a remarkable feat.

A CARD TRICK

One of my hypnotic subjects at Worcester said, "I don't like to do this trick. It gives me a terrible headache. I think you ought to know about it, though." He said, "Go into a drugstore and buy a deck of cards. Open it. Take out all the jokers and extra cards." Then he said, "Shuffle the deck thoroughly, half a dozen times, and cut it and shuffle it again. Deal the cards, face up, one at a time, and then turn them over." Then he said, "Pick up those cards, shuffle them again and deal them back side up." And he named the cards in the exact order back side up. He had placed them face up and then turned them over.

Then he showed me. You bought a pack of cards with cross lines and little squares on the back. The squares are not cut truly. He said, "All I had to do was to remember a quarter of a square missing here, a quarter missing there on another card. I just remembered fifty-two cards. And it always has given me a terrible headache—and it took long, hard practice to do it!" He had used that in working his way through school. He had earned a lot of money that way.

It really is amazing what people can do. Only they don't know what they can do.

11. Treating Psychotic Patients

In dealing with psychotics, Erickson did not attempt to solve all of the patient's problems. As with other patients, he tried to bring about small changes that could lead to larger and broader ones. Since people who are undergoing psychotic reactions usually respond in a "black and white," extreme manner, Erickson's interventions with them are often most obvious and the results most immediate. Erickson's first psychiatric experiences took place in a mental hospital, and he may have developed some of his important principles of therapy from work with psychotic patients. Certainly, this must have been true of two of his favorite maxims, "Speak in the patient's language," and "Join the patient."

In situations where others might have persisted in doggedly attempting to "get a history" or to "reason" with the patient, Erickson often introduced an unexpected element. As we see in "The Patient Who Stood" and "Herbert," he would often lead the patient to a point where he is forced to take a direct action and make a choice.

In this section, we will see examples of these, as well as of other therapeutic approaches, including the use of effective manipulations and reframing.

INSIDE OUT

At Worcester I had a patient who always returned your greeting. If you asked him a question, he looked at you brightly. He was gentle, docile, very quiet. He went to the mess hall, went to bed, was orderly, had nothing to say. He said "Hello" or "Goodbye."

I got tired of trying to interview him. I wanted his history. And he was obviously in a world of unreality. It took me quite a while to figure out how to get into his world.

One day I walked up to him and said, "Hello." He said, "Hello." Then I took off my jacket, turned it inside out, and put it on backwards.

Then I took his jacket off, turned it inside out, put it on him backwards, and said, "I'd like to have you tell me your story."

I got a history. Join the patient.

Erickson symbolically entered into the patient's "inside-out" and "backwards" world of "unreality" when he turned his own jacket inside out and backwards. He then made the patient join him in using the same "language." Once the two of them were in the same "world" (inside-out and backwards), they could talk to one another.

Incidentally, the fact that the patient "always returned your greeting" was a good indicator that he was likely to imitate the therapist's behavior.

THE PATIENT WHO STOOD

There was a patient standing around the ward for six or seven years. He didn't talk. He'd go to the cafeteria. He'd come back, go to bed when told, go to the bathroom when he needed to. But for the most part he stood.

You could talk to him by the hour without getting a response. One day I made certain he would make a response. I approached him with a floor polisher. A floor polisher has a twelve-by-twelve beam of wood, about three feet long, with a long handle attached.

It is covered with an old rug and you push it back and forth to polish the floor.

I took one of those floor polishers over to him, wrapped his fingers around the handle. He stood there. Every day I'd tell him, "Move that floor polisher."

So he began moving it an inch back and forth. Each day I would increase the length that he would push the floor polisher, until I had him going clear around the ward, hour after hour. And he began talking. He began accusing me of abusing him by making him polish the floor all day long.

I told him, "If you want to do something else, I'm perfectly willing." And so he began making beds. And he began talking, giving his history, expressing his delusions. And pretty soon I was able to give him ground privileges.

He walked around the hospital grounds. And within a year's time he was able to go home and work, and visit for a week, two weeks, three weeks, a month.

He was still psychotic but he could adjust to the outside world.

Here Erickson is illustrating the principle of initiating a small change and of gradually extending that change. We have seen this in many situations, particularly in his treatment of phobics. He also is demonstrating that he would direct a patient until the patient was able to take over for himself. I have heard Erickson say to a patient, "Until you do, I will do." In this case the patient was directed until he finally broke his silence to complain of abuse. When he was able to "do for himself," that is, to speak, Erickson offers him "another alternative." The ability to make choices was the first real indication that the patient was becoming healthier.

TWO JESUS CHRISTS

I had two Jesus Christs on the ward. And they spent the entire day explaining, "I am Jesus Christ." They buttonholed everybody and explained, "I am the *real* Jesus Christ."

And so I put John and Alberto on a bench and told them, "You sit there. Now, each of you tells me you're Jesus Christ. Now, John, I want you to explain to Alberto that *you*, not he, are Jesus Christ. Alberto, you tell John, *you* are the real Jesus Christ and that he is not; you are."

I kept them sitting on that bench, explaining to each other all day long that they were the true Jesus Christ. And after about a month, John said, "I'm Jesus Christ and that crazy Alberto says that he is Jesus Christ."

I said to John, "You know, John, you say the same thing that he says. And he says the same things that you say. Now, I think that one of you is crazy, because there is only one Jesus Christ."

John thought that over for a week. He said, "I'm saying the same things as that crazy fool is saying. He's crazy and I'm saying what he says. That must mean I'm crazy too; and I don't want to be crazy."

I said, "Well, I don't think you're Jesus Christ. And you don't want to be crazy. I'll have you work in the hospital library." He worked there a few days and came to me and said, "There's something awfully wrong: every book has my name on every page." He opened a book, showed me JOHN THORNTON; on every page he found his name.

I agreed and showed him how on every page MILTON ERICKSON appeared. I had him help me find Dr. Hugh Carmichael's name, Jim Glitton's name, Dave Shakow's name. In fact, we could find any name he thought of on that page.

John said, "These letters don't belong to a name; they belong to that *word!*"

I said, "That's right."

John continued working in the library. Six months later, he went home free of his psychotic identifications.

Erickson does not rely on ordinary methods of "persuasion" but, instead, in both instances, places John into situations where he can discover for himself that his ideas are delusional. Erickson relies on the technique of "mirroring" the patients' behavior. In the first example, Erickson arranges for the delusion to be mirrored by another patient, who, conveniently, happens to suffer from the same delusion. In the second situation, Erickson himself mirrors the behavior, by finding his own name on the page. This "mirroring" approach is utilized by Robert Lindner in his classic story "The Jet-Propelled Couch." Erickson once told me that Lindner had been his student and had consulted with him before publishing his book The Fifty-Minute Hour, *which contains this story. The story is about a therapist whose patient lived in delusional worlds. When the therapist belabors the patient with excited tales about his own "trips" and experiences in those worlds, when he joins the patient in his delusions, the patient assumes the therapist's role and tries to show him that the type of thinking in which they both had immersed themselves is, indeed, delusional.*

HERBERT

When I first went to Rhode Island State Hospital, I had a job on the male ward, and there was a patient named Herbert who had been there for nearly a year. Before being committed to the hospital, Herbert weighted 240 pounds, was a manual laborer, and spent his time playing cards or working. He lived to work and to play cards.

He had become depressed, very seriously depressed. He began losing weight and was finally committed to Rhode Island State Hospital where, for at least four months, he had weighed only eighty pounds. He was being fed 4,000 calories a day by tube feeding without gaining.

Of course, I inherited Herbert as my patient; the other doctors were sick and tired of tube-feeding Herbert. I was a new doctor, and young, so I got the dirty work. The first time I tube-fed Herbert, I cut his tube-feeding down to 2,500 calories. I thought that was enough for an eighty-pound man.

When I tube-fed Herbert, he said, "Are you as crazy as the other doctors? Are you going to play that same lousy trick on me that all the others do, pretending to give me a tube-feeding? I know you're bringing me a tube-feeding; I can see it. But you're all magicians and in some way you make it disappear, as if you were Houdini! And I never get fed anything! You just put the tube down through my nose, and you *say* you tube-feed me, but actually you haven't, 'cause I ain't got no stomach."

I listened to Herbert. His depression had resulted in a sour, acid, sardonic view of life. When he told me he didn't have a stomach, I told him, "I think you *have* a stomach."

He said, "You're just as loony as the other doctors! Why do they have loony doctors in a crazy house? Maybe that's the best place for crazy doctors, in a crazy house."

So, every tube-feeding for a week I told Herbert, "Next week, on Monday morning, you're going to prove to me that you've got a stomach."

He said, "You're hopeless. You're crazier than the other patients around here. You think I'm going to prove I've got a stomach, when I ain't got no stomach."

On that Monday morning, I fixed Herbert's tube-feeding— half milk, half cream, raw eggs, baking soda, vinegar, and raw cod liver oil. Now, when you tube-feed a person, you shove a column of air the length of the tube into the stomach. That's why you pour continuously, to avoid shoving more columns of air.

I gave him his feeding, shoving *many* columns of air into his stomach. I withdrew the tube, stood there waiting, and Herbert burped, and said, "Rotten fish."

I said, *"You* said that, Herbert. *You* know you burped; you know it was rotten fish. You could only burp because you've got a stomach, so you proved to me you've got a stomach, by burping." And Herbert kept on burping!

He told me, "You think you're smart, don't you?"

I agreed with him.

Now, Herbert did his sleeping standing up. I didn't know that a human being could sleep standing up, but I checked up on Herbert. The attendants were afraid to put him in bed, because Herbert fought so furiously; they let him have his way. I went down at 1 and 2 and 3 A.M., and found Herbert, sound asleep, standing up on the ward.

So I told Herbert every day for a week, "Herbert, you're going to prove to me you can sleep lying down."

Herbert said, "You're hopeless; you've got more delusions than you can shake a stick at."

And then the next week, every day, I asked Herbert if he ever took a bath, or ever took a shower. Herbert was very insulted by that question. Of course he took a bath; he took a shower. Any man in his right mind takes a bath, "What's wrong with you, that you don't know that?"

"I just thought I'd inquire."

He said, "Do you have to inquire every day?"

I said, "Well, I need to, because you think you can't sleep lying down, and you've got to prove to me that you can sleep lying down."

Herbert said, "There is no hope for you at all."

So, one evening, the next week, I took Herbert to the hydrotherapy room, and had him lie in the continuous bathtub. That's a bathtub with a canvas hammock. Your body is greased with Vaseline; you lie down and a cover is put over the tub. Only your head remains above the cover. You are lying down in the bathtub, and water, at body temperature, flows continuously over your body. Now, when that happens to you, you go to sleep! There's nothing else you can do.

The next morning I awakened Herbert. I said, "Herbert, I told you you would prove to me you could sleep lying down."

Herbert said, "You're a smart aleck."

I said, "And you were able to sleep in bed." Herbert slept in bed thereafter.

When I got his weight up to 110 pounds, I said, "Herbert, I'm tired of tube-feeding you. Next week, you're going to *drink* your tube feeding."

Herbert said, "I can't swallow; I don't know how."

I said, "Herbert, next week, on Monday, you're going to be the first man at the mess-hall door. You'll be pounding on the door and yelling at the attendants, 'Open the door!' because you'll want a glass of milk, a glass of water. I will have water and milk on one of the tables, and you will really want them."

Herbert said, "I think you're incurable! Too bad, a young man like you in a state hospital, with crazy people. And *so* young. And *so* crazy."

I told him for a week that he was going to be pounding on the mess-hall door crying that he wanted a glass of milk, a glass of water. And Herbert really thought I was off my rocker.

On Sunday night, Herbert went to bed. I had the attendant spread-eagle him so that he was tied down by the hands and the feet, and couldn't get out of bed. And I had given him his evening tube feeding with plenty of table salt in it.

Herbert got thirsty during the night—very, very thirsty. When he was released, in the morning, he rushed to the water fountain, but the water was turned off. He rushed to the toilet, to drink out of the toilet bowl, but the water had been turned off. He rushed to the mess-hall door, pounded on the door and yelled at the attendant, "Open these doors! I gotta have that water! I've gotta have that milk!"

He drank it.

When I came on the ward, Herbert said, "You think you're smart."

I said, "You told me that before. I agreed with you then and I agree with you now."

Herbert drank milk and soup. But he held out that he could not swallow solid food. When he was up to 115 pounds I told Herbert, "Next week, you're going to swallow solid food."

Herbert said, "You're a lot crazier than I ever thought. I can't swallow solid food."

I said, "Next week you will."

Now, how did I make him swallow solid food?

I knew that Herbert had once been a small child. I knew *I* had been. I knew that all people were once small children and that they all had human nature. I just employed human nature. Now, all of you know something of human nature. How would you make Herbert swallow solid food?

I had Herbert sit down at a table, with a plate full of food in front of him. On one side was a deteriorated patient and on the other side was a deteriorated patient. And they never ate food from their plates. They always ate from somebody *else's* plate. And Herbert knew that his plate was *his*. But the only way he could *keep* it his was by swallowing it! He didn't want those damn crazy fools to eat *his* food! That's human nature.

After he'd eaten his first solid-food meal, I asked Herbert how he liked his dinner. He answered, "I didn't like it but I *had* to eat it. It was mine."

I said, "I told you that you could swallow solid food."

He said, "You think you're smart."

I said, "Herbert, that's getting repetitious. I've agreed with you twice before. I'm still agreeing with you."

Herbert walked away, swearing at me.

When he weighed 120 pounds I said, "Herbert, you're eating solid food, gaining weight."

Herbert said, "I only eat because I *have* to. Because if I don't you'll put me between those two crazy idiots."

I said, "That's right."

"I ain't got no appetite. I don't like what I have to swallow. I have to swallow to keep those idiots from stealing it."

I said, "Well, Herbert, you're going to find out you *do* have an appetite and you *do* get hungry. Now, it's January, in Rhode Island. It's cold weather. I'll have you dressed properly. I'm going to send you out to the hospital farm, without lunch. There's an oak tree, fifteen feet in diameter, that I want you to chop down and reduce to kindling wood. That will work up an appetite for you."

Herbert said, "I'll sublet that contract."

I said, "Even so, you'll be out on the farm all day without a lunch. And in the evening when you return, you'll discover that you are hungry."

Herbert said, "You *are* a dreamer."

After I sent Herbert out on the farm, I went to the chef and said, "Mrs. Walsh, you weigh 350 pounds. You like your food. Now, Mrs. Walsh, I want you to skip breakfast and lunch. I want you to go hungry. Then for dinner, I want you to prepare twice as much as you can eat of your favorite foods. And you can look forward to gorging yourself on all your favorite foods. And be very, very generous. Prepare twice as much as you can possibly eat. I'll tell you where to set up the table."

Herbert came in from the farm. I put him into a corner, had a table set up in front of him. I had places for two put on the table. Mrs. Walsh was on one side. Herbert was looking at her and the table. Mrs. Walsh brought out the food in huge bowlfuls. She began eating ravenously.

Herbert watched her eat, and got hungrier and hungrier. Finally he said, "Can I have some?"

She said, "Sure."

Herbert ate, because he was hungry. My daughters, when we have a family dinner, always go out and give the dogs their bones. They always say, "The way the dogs gnaw at those bones makes my mouth water. And I want to gnaw on the same bones."

Poor Herbert. His mouth began watering, watching Mrs. Walsh.

On the ward that evening, Herbert said, "You really *are* smart."

I said, "At last you found that out! Now, Herbert, there's one thing more I'm going to do for you. You used to play cards. You've been in the hospital nearly a year and you haven't once played cards. Nobody's been able to persuade you to play cards. Now, tonight, you're going to play cards."

Herbert said, "You're crazier than ever! There *is* no hope for you."

I said, "There's hope for *you*, Herbert; you're going to play cards, tonight."

He said, "That'll be the day!"

That evening two tall, husky attendants on each side of him led him up to a table with four cardplayers, who were very deteriorated mentally. One played poker. One played bridge. One played pinochle. They'd deal out the cards, and each would take a turn throwing down a card. One would say, "I take that one; I have a full house." Another would say, "I trump that." The next might announce, "That's thirty points for me." And they played cards continuously all day.

Now, Herbert was forced to stand there, between the two attendants, and watch that card game. Finally, he said, "Get me away from these idiots. I'll play poker with you if you'll let me get away from here. I can't stand what they're doing with the cards."

Later that evening I came on the ward and watched Herbert play cards. Herbert said, "You won again."

I said, "*You* won."

A few months later Herbert was discharged from the hospital. He regained weight, to my knowledge, up to 180 pounds, and worked every day. All I did for him was correct his symptoms. I put him into a situation where he corrected his symptoms.

Erickson uses the modality and the setting of a mental hospital to convey ways of getting people to want to do things.

The principle is either to force the subject to stick with a situation, often by repeating the subject's own words, or, as in the case of Herbert, to use more complicated psychological binds. Erickson proved to Herbert that his concepts were incorrect. He proved to Herbert that Herbert did have a stomach, by forcing him to burp. He proved to him that he could sleep lying down instead of just standing up, by putting him into a continuous-bath tub. He proved to him that he could swallow, by making him so thirsty that he had to drink liquids and had to beg for them. He proved to him that he could voluntarily eat solid food by placing it between two deteriorated patients who would steal the food off his plate—unless Herbert ate it. He proved to him that he had an appetite for food, by arranging with Mrs. Walsh to eat ravenously in front of him. Finally, he provoked in Herbert the desire to play cards, by exposing him to some mentally deteriorated card players, until Herbert promised, "I'll play poker with you if you'll let me get away from here. I can't stand what they're doing with the cards." Thus, he led Herbert to discover that Herbert did really want to see cards played correctly. In other words, Herbert learned that he had a desire for good card playing.

Erickson, rather modestly, sums up by saying, "All I did for him was correct his symptoms. I put him into a situation where he corrected his symptoms." Actually, by correcting one symptom after another, Erickson evoked behavior patterns, ways of thinking and responding, that led Herbert to recognize that he had an appetite for life as well as for food. And once he started playing cards he could not help becoming aware that he had a social sense and a desire to interact with other people.

How did Erickson force people to respond in certain desired ways? With Herbert it is clear that he used his knowledge of ordinary human responses—competitiveness, tendency to imitate (as in developing an appetite when with the voracious eater). He also used "cognitive" approaches, as when he forced Herbert into a situation in which he could not fail to recognize, cognitively, that he must have a stomach—in order to burp.

Of course, Herbert was treated in a mental hospital, where Erickson could exert almost absolute control over his behavior. However, Erickson is illustrating the use of the psychological bind. In the psychological bind, just as in the physical bind, the patient is put into a situation that will inevitably lead to the desired result. In this case, Herbert responded, as predicted, to each challenging situation. It was as if Erickson was playing pool and had called his shots. This must inevitably impress a patient with the therapist's ability to help him.

In this treatment, Erickson deals with one symptom at a time. He starts off in a relatively peripheral area, and once he makes a change in that symptom, he works toward more central symptoms. Each success is predicated on the fact that there was a previous success.

12. Manipulation and Future Orientation

In his keynote address to the International Congress on Ericksonian Approaches to Hypnosis and Psychotherapy, December 7, 1980, Jay Haley said, "Erickson was really quite comfortable with power. You know, there was a period when people thought there was something wrong with power, but that wasn't his point of view. He didn't mind taking it or using it. I recall him saying that he was on a panel and 'There was no power there so I took over the panel.' With his willingness to take and use power, I think it is fortunate that he was a benevolent man. If the kind of influence he had was turned to destructive purposes, it would have been most unfortunate. He was not only benevolent, but he was consistently helpful to people, both in and out of his office. . . . I never had a doubt about his ethics or his benevolent intentions and I wasn't concerned about his exploiting anyone for any personal advantage."

It is important to keep Erickson's "benevolence" in mind when we consider his love of practical jokes. Practical jokes are often used to express thinly disguised hostility, yet in the Erickson family, the "victim" was as amused as the "perpetrator." The victim is certainly not harmed, although there might be an argument in some situations as to who is the victim. But there is no indication that any of the Erickson jokes originate from or express hostility.

In this chapter, the stories are told as models for "setting up" situations to achieve a planned purpose. In many cases, practical jokes and humorous stories can be seen as prototypes of Erickson's scheme of therapy. When Erickson practiced therapy, just as when he told or set up a practical joke, he knew the ending. The patient did not. Erickson began with a goal in mind—that of changing the patient's responses from "sick" or self-destructive to "healthier" or constructive. As the therapist, he manipulated the situation to actualize the goal. Many techniques were used to maintain and build up the interest and motivation of the patient —challenges, stimulation of curiosity, diversionary tactics, and humor.

The essential element in Erickson's practical jokes was not hostility, but surprise. In his therapy, also, the patient was often surprised, both at "prescriptions" and at his own responses. And, just as the listener experiences a sense of relief at hearing the punch line after the buildup of suspense, the patient was relieved to hear a clear-cut prescription.

Erickson felt that shock and surprise were useful in breaking up rigid mental sets. The surprise did not have to be administered in a sophisticated way. During my first visit with him, in the middle of our conversation, he reached into a drawer and pulled out a small tricycle horn. He squeezed the ball three or four times —toot, toot, toot—and commented, "Surprise always helps." At the time this seemed a juvenile thing for him to do, and didn't seem to have any particular effect on me. However, in retrospect, I believe it contributed to the general atmosphere that enabled me to enter a hypnotic trance and to respond to his suggestions. It kept me off-balance and introduced an element from childhood that he may have used to evoke the childhood memories I was trying to recall.

"Future Orientation" has been included in this chapter because it seems to fit in with planning, and with "manipulation" in the sense in which Erickson uses this word. In the first story, *"manipulation" is used where others might use such concepts as "mastery," "effective action," or "managing." A positive attitude toward the future is the best antidote to depression or obsessive thinking—and this is true of the anticipation of amusement at the culmination of a practical joke as well as of the expectation that the passing of time will bring growth.*

MANIPULATION

I've been accused of manipulating patients—to which I reply: Every mother manipulates her baby—if she wants it to live. And every time you go to the store you manipulate the clerk to do your bidding. And when you go to a restaurant, you manipulate the waiter. And the teacher in school manipulates you into learning to read and write. In fact, life is one big manipulation. The final manipulation is putting you to rest. And *that's* manipulation, too.

They have to lower the coffin and then they have to get the ropes out—all manipulation.

And you manipulate a pencil—to write, to record thoughts. And you manipulate yourself, carrying around Planters peanuts, or cigarettes, or Life Savers. One of my daughters called them "mint-pepper saferlifes." She also says "flutterbys" and "melon-waters." And now she's pregnant and living in Dallas.

I wrote a letter to her, saying that naming the baby would be easy. All she has to do, if it is a boy, is to name it "Dallas." If it is a girl she could name it "Alice." Her husband says that in Texas you have to have double names. He wants to name it "Billy-Rubin." You know what bilirubin is? A bile secretion! Of course, he could call it "Hemo Globin."

Erickson stressed that, in all situations, you must manipulate. Paul Watzlawick pointed out, in The Language of Change, *"One cannot not influence." Every communication must evoke* responses and is, therefore, a manipulation. So, you might as well manipulate effectively, relevantly, and constructively. In this brief story, Erickson gives examples of manipulation from birth to death. He comes full-circle with another birth, and the cycle continues. He is telling his daughter Roxy, who used to play with words, that she can still playfully manipulate words in naming her child. He is also telling her, and us, that we should not lose the playfulness and spontaneity of childhood.

Erickson instructed therapists in ways of setting up stories. He said, "One thing I teach my students is this: Take a new book by an author who you know is good. Read the last chapter first. Speculate about the contents of the preceding chapter. Speculate in all possible directions. You will be wrong in a lot of your speculations. Read that chapter and then speculate on the previous chapter. You read a good book from the last chapter to the first, speculating all the way."

Erickson stated that this was not only a good way to learn to set up a story, but it was also an effective way of learning how to speculate freely—in all directions. "And you break your pattern of rigid thinking. It is extremely useful."

Through his tales he is suggesting that we, the readers, can determine our goals and then devise strategies to achieve these goals. The next stories, about his son Bert, are good illustrations of the Ericksons' love of practical jokes. Through their humorous element and from the relish with which Erickson told them, these stories model an optimistic and humorous view of life.

BERT AND COCOA

This was when Bert was transferred to Camp Pendleton, California, where Betty had some relatives. We thought he might look up some of them sometime. And one morning, at 3 A.M., Bert, in his fatigues, knocked on the door of a house by the roadside. The man of the house came to the door and saw the young marine, who said, "I beg your pardon, sir. I have a message for your wife, sir. Will you call your wife to the door, please, sir?"

He said, "Can't you give me the message?"

Bert said, "The message, sir, is for your wife, sir. Will you please call her to the door so I can give it to her, sir?"

Bert got into the kitchen, and said to the man's wife, "Ma'am, I was walking down the highway returning to Camp Pendleton and got to thinking about my mom. That made me homesick for my Mom and for the kind of cocoa my mom makes. And I know it would please my mom if I gave somebody her recipe. I'll make cocoa the way my mom does."

That man kept thinking, "Shall I call the police, men in white, shore patrol?"

Bert made the cocoa, talking about generalities. When the cocoa was nearly ready, he said, "Do you have children, ma'am?"

She said, "Yes, three girls."

"How old are they, ma'am? Oh, young. Cocoa is good for growing children. Would you call them into the kitchen so they can drink some of this cocoa like my mom makes?"

So she went and called three little girls and Bert clowned around a bit for the little girls, stirring the cocoa with a spoon held over his back. Anything to please the kids. And when the cocoa was poured, Bert took a sip, sighed deeply and said, "Yes siree sir, its just like the cocoa my mom makes. I get so homesick for my mom."

"Where does your mother live?"

"She lives in Detroit. I get so homesick for my mom and her cocoa."

"What is your mother's name?"

"It's Elizabeth."

"I meant her *last* name."

"Why ma'am, she has a middle name in front of her last name."

"What is your mother's middle name?"

"Euphemia."

And the woman said, "Elizabeth Euphemia? Egad, what is *your* name?"

"It's Erickson, cousin Anita."

About a year later we happened to visit our cousin Anita in California, and they told us about that.

AUTHORIZATION

Bert was nineteen and living in Michigan. We were living in Phoenix. He wrote and said, "I want to buy a car, and I've got to get documents signed because I'm a minor." I wrote back, "Honestly, Bert, I can't really sign an authorization for you to get a car because I can't take the responsibility. I'm living in Arizona and you're in Michigan. Now, Michigan has a good population. Surely you can find some businessman with a good reputation who will sign it for you."

He wrote later that he walked into a certain man's office and said, "I'm only nineteen. I want to buy a car. My father is in Arizona; he can't sign an authorization. I'd like to have you sign for me."

The man said, "Are you out of your mind?"

Bert said, "No, sir. You can think the matter over. You will know that I am very much in my mind."

The man said, "That's right, you are. Give me that paper." He was the chief of police in Ann Arbor!

Bert knew he couldn't park his car one-half inch out of the way or drive one-half mile per hour over the speed limit. The first time he drove into Detroit a traffic officer waved him to a stop, came over, and said, "So you are Bert Erickson. I recognized your car immediately and I am delighted to see what Bert Erickson looks like."

Then he was driving in northern Michigan with some friends. A siren sounded behind him. A motorcycle patrolman had sounded the siren, so Bert pulled over to the side of the road and his friend said, "What do you suppose has gone wrong?" Bert said, "Nothing."

A patrolman came alongside of the car and said, "So you are Bert Erickson. I recognized your car immediately and I wanted to see what that one looked like who asked the police chief to sign for him."

Bert obviously knows that the person who might take responsibility for authorizing him to drive a car is the same person who has the power to take away this authorization, if Bert should fail to live up to his part of the agreement. Obviously, he is declaring his belief that he will not break any laws and has the nerve to approach the chief of police for this authorization.

The message in this story could be that one need not fear authority. One can, in fact, engage or utilize authority in the fulfillment of one's goals. The authority is seen as being responsive to an effective approach. Another message is that people will respond positively when approached in an unorthodox or an unusual way. The policemen who stopped Bert are bemused by his approach to their supreme authority. The unorthodox commands attention. Also, by taking an unorthodox approach, one can frequently bypass the conventional barriers that have been set up by society—such as the red tape involved in getting a license. On an intrapsychic level, by approaching and working out some type of a deal with our "inner authorities," we can bypass the strictures we have set up to maintain our own equilibrium or neurotic structure.

DOLORES

One day in June, Bert wrote us from Michigan and ended the letter with "As I close this letter, I've got to meet Dolores." Now, Bert always had a secret, and we knew better than to ask who Dolores was.

Every week or so we got a letter with a one-line mention of Dolores.

"I had dinner with Dolores," or "I'm going to call on Dolores." "I got some socks I know Dolores will like." At the same time he kept up a similar correspondence with my father in Milwaukee, and my father knew better than to ask questions.

In August, Bert wrote, "I ought to send you both some pictures of Dolores." He said that to my father too. So we waited. In September, Bert wrote us, "I hope Grandpa and Grandma will like Dolores. I'm sure *you* would and I've figured out a way for Grandpa and Grandma to meet Dolores. I'll go there for Thanksgiving Day dinner."

Now, Bert had a marvelous gift: He could cross his eyes, stand pigeon-toed, his arms seeming to be barely attached, and get a silly grin on his face that was irritating to look at. It made you want to slap his face. He showed up on Milwaukee at 1 A.M. on a very cold Thanksgiving Day. He came in the house and my father said, "Where is Dolores?"

He looked sillier than ever. "I had trouble getting her on the plane. She isn't dressed. She's outside!"

"Why is she outside?"

"She isn't dressed."

My mother said, "I'll get a bathrobe." My father said, "You go and bring that girl in."

Bert came in carrying a huge box, obviously heavy. "This was the only way I could get her on the plane. She isn't properly dressed."

"Open that box, boy."

He opened it and there was Dolores—one turkey, one goose —both named Dolores. And Grandpa and Grandma liked Dolores! That had been going on since June!

Don't ever trust the Ericksons.

GETTING JEFF TO CALL

My daughter Kristi went to a basketball game at North High when she was fifteen. She was a student in West High and she went to North High with a companion, Margie, a girl she had met in kindergarten. When she came home, she said to me, "Guess who I saw at the game tonight? You remember the little kid up the street who moved away and we often wondered what happened to him? He's a senior in North High. He has three athletic letters, and good grades. And now my only problem is to get him to date me, and let him think the whole idea is his own."

I remembered that kid very well. Three basketball games later, Kristi came into the bedroom and said, "Jeff doesn't know it, but he's going to call me tomorrow afternoon for a date."

I was alert to the telephone and so was she. On Saturday afternoon, the phone rang and Jeff asked her for a date. I waited patiently to find out how she'd managed that. You don't rush things. So, after waiting for a while, I said, "How did you maneuver that?"

She said, "Margie was too shy to introduce me, so at the next basketball game, I looked him up and said, 'I'll bet you don't know me,' and he looked me up and down and said, 'That's right, I don't.' So I told him, 'I'm one of the Erickson girls—which one?' "

He looked her over and said, "Kristi."

She said, "That's right. It's nice seeing you again after all these years." And then she said, "I have to go and find Margie," and walked off—the old trick of letting the audience cry for more. She walked off before he had the chance to ask any questions. He was asking for more, but she was gone.

At the next meeting she saw him in a crowd, talking earnestly to another boy. She sneaked up, close enough to get the trend of the conversation, and then she evaporated, and when Jeff wandered off she walked over to that boy and started the same conversation. No introductions. They just discussed that problem, whatever it was.

At the third basketball game, Kristi hunted up that student and listened to the conversation, and Jeff came around and the other boy said, "Hi, Jeff, let me introduce you to—oh, my, *we* haven't been introduced yet." "Guess you'll have to do it," she told Jeff.

That's when my daughter said, "Jeff is calling tomorrow for a date."

Kristi cleverly gives Jeff enough information and enough contact with her to arouse his interest, but not to satisfy it. He is left wanting more. She has him introduce her to one of his friends, someone he respects, who obviously is interested in her. He is, of necessity, brought back to recall his warm associations with her during childhood and, at the same time, to see her in a different light—that is, as someone who is a peer and is attractive to a young man. This also arouses his jealousy and competitive instincts. Therefore, Kristi is quite certain that he will soon call.

Why did Erickson include sentences such as "They just discussed that problem"? This does not fit into a conversation be-

*tween two adolescents. Was he leaving room for a patient or
reader to put his own "problem" into the tale?*

WHAT WOULD YOU DO IF
I SLAMMED YOU?

When my daughter Betty Alice was signing a school contract,
the members of the school board were holding their breath. Their
sighs were released when she finished her signature. Betty Alice
wondered what that meant. She knew it wouldn't take long to
find out. She did find out very promptly. The class that she taught
was composed of fifteen-year-old delinquents, waiting for their
sixteenth birthday so they could quit school, and they all had long
lists of arrests. They were *really* delinquents. One of them had
been arrested at least thirty times and he had twice beaten up a
policeman. And he was six feet two inches tall and weighed 220
pounds. The previous semester he had approached the teacher
and said, "Miss Johnson, what would you do if I slammed you?"
Apparently the teacher gave him the wrong answer because he
slammed her across the room and put her in the hospital. Betty
Alice thought to herself, "I wonder when that poor kid will tangle
with me. I am five foot two and weigh 102 pounds." She didn't
have to wait long.

She was riding her bike in the park when she saw him. "Here
was this great big giant with a nasty smile on his face, so I put
a wondering look on my face and opened my big blue eyes widely.
He stopped in front of me, and asked, 'What would you do if I
slammed you?' "

The poor kid. She took two quick steps toward him and
snarled, "So help me God, I'd kill you!" He'd asked a simple
question; she'd given a simple reply, "So help me God, I'd kill
you, so get on over to that seat quick!"

He had never heard such a loud snarl from such a little kitten. As he was sitting down, there was this wondering look on his face. She had put him down and he knew he wouldn't dare let any *other* kid harass her. He was her constant protector. It was so beautiful. She was very beautiful. The unexpected always helps. You never do what's expected.

The next two vignettes further illustrate this dictum.

DACHSHUND AND GERMAN SHEPHERD

One of my students was less than five feet and she asked me if she had done right. She was taking her little puppy, a dachshund, out for a walk one evening. A big German shepherd came roaring down the alley, swearing at her and the puppy, declaring his intent to eat them alive. She grabbed up the puppy and charged the German shepherd, yelling at him. He turned around and went goggy-eyed and ran back home. Because it's when you do the unexpected thing that you cause a lot of rearrangement in a person's thinking.

DERAIL THEM

I got a letter yesterday from a former student. He said, "I had a rather paranoid patient in the room. All he wanted to talk about was *his* ideas. I tried to get his attention, but couldn't. Then I thought about the unexpected, so I said, "No, I don't like eating liver either." The patient paused, shook his head, and said, "Usually, I like chicken." And then the patient began talking about his real problems. The unexpected can always derail a train of thought, a trend of behavior, and you ought to use it.

I know that in college and in medical school, when I was an intern, whenever a professor wanted to reprimand me, I always came up with an idiotic irrelevant question or statement—and derailed them. In the summer time a professor began: "Erickson, I don't like . . ."

"I don't like the snow either," I said.

Then he would say, "What are you talking about?"

I said, "The snow."

"What snow?"

"The marvelous wonder—that no two snowflakes are the same."

I think therapists ought to have ready, at any time, some irrelevant remarks. Then when patients sit down, saying a whole chapter that is irrelevant, get them off that conversational track. Derail them by some irrelevant remark. For example, "I know what you are thinking. I like trains too."

Erickson always made certain that he, not the patient, controlled the therapeutic sessions. Karen Horney once said, "Patients enter therapy, not to cure their neuroses, but to perfect them." If patients are to determine what happens in a therapeutic session, almost all of them will unconsciously do whatever is necessary to prevent real therapeutic change. Therefore, when the patient is on a useless track, it is important that the therapist derail him and direct him to a more fruitful one.

LANCE AND COOKIE

The Erickson family is very fond of practical jokes that do not hurt. They are remembered long and happily.

At a student dance at Ann Arbor, my son Lance saw a girl who looked attractive to him, so he cut in on her and asked her for a date. She told him firmly and gently, "The answer is no; I'm going steady."

Lance said, "Oh, I don't mind that a bit."

"The answer is no."

A month later he saw the same girl, cut in on her at a dance, and asked for a date. The girl said, "You asked me that once before. The answer was no then and it still is no."

Lance said, "That means we'll have to discuss it over a table at Oscar's Restaurant."

She looked at him as if she thought he was out of his mind.

But Lance did thorough research. One Saturday afternoon he and his best friend walked into the nursing students' dormitory parlor, where this girl was entertaining her boyfriend. Lance walked up to the girl and said, "Cookie, I want you to meet my best friend, Dean." "Dean, this is my cousin Cookie. Only I'm not really her cousin. I'm her illegitimate half-cousin. But we don't make much mention of that outside the family." Then he asked, "How's Uncle George's broken leg?"

The girl knew she had an Uncle George in northern Michigan with a broken leg.

Then he added, "How many quarts of strawberries did Aunt Nellie can last summer?" And the girl knew she had an Aunt Nellie whose hobby was canning strawberries. Then he asked, "How is Vicki getting along with her algebra in high school?" And Cookie knew all about Vicki's troubles in high school.

Then Lance happened to notice the boyfriend with his mouth open, eyes popping. He said, "Do you know Cookie? My name is Lance. I'm Cookie's cousin, only I'm not really her cousin. I'm her illegitimate half-cousin. We don't make much mention of that outside the family." Then he turned to Dean and said, "Dean, why don't you take him out to dinner?"

And Dean walked over, put his arm around the young man. And Lance turned to Cookie and said, "We've got a lot of family news to exchange."

In all the years that we've known Cookie she has never raised her voice: she's calm and gentle and firm. And Cookie said, "There are a lot of things I want to say to you." But she didn't notice that they had walked into that restaurant.

When they got engaged, Cookie wanted a picture of him, so he gave her one. I had taken that picture myself, when he was a little kid, in the nude.

And one day he said, "Cookie, I really ought to meet your parents."

And Cookie said, "Oh, oh, oh, oh. I suppose you'll have to."

One afternoon at four o'clock, a well-dressed young man carrying a briefcase walked into the Cooks' backyard and said, "Mr. Cook, I want to discuss insurance with you." Lance has a gift of gab. He can discuss lightning insurance, tornado insurance, life insurance, accident insurance, car insurance. At quarter to five Mrs. Cook came out on the back porch and called to her husband, "Supper."

Lance turned to Mr. Cook and in a small voice said, "You know it's a long time since I had a home-cooked meal. I'm certain your wife wouldn't mind setting an extra plate for me. It really would be delightful to have a home-cooked meal."

They got into the house, and Lance said, "Mrs. Cook, it's been a long time since I had a home-cooked meal. Your husband assured me it would be no trouble at all to set an extra plate. I'm willing to take pot luck."

Right through the meal, Lance discussed everything. He complimented every dish and Mrs. Cook looked daggers at Mr. Cook. At the end of the meal, Lance expressed his gratitude and then he said, "I have one more insurance policy, and this one is one I know you'll want to buy. It's an insurance policy against an undesirable son-in-law!"

Lance and Cookie both remembered this incident when I asked them about it, in 1980. Lance recalled that after he had

*delivered his punch line, Mr. Cook turned to Cookie with a smile
and said, "Why, you little shit!"*

*Just as Lance was confident that he could induce Cookie to
date him and to marry him, Erickson was supremely confident
that patients would do what he asked. He was also confident that
his therapy would succeed. This confidence was not based on
wishful thinking, but on years of experience, careful observation,
and painstaking preparation.*

*The case histories that follow demonstrate some of the results
of this planning, which was at least as thorough as the planning
for one of his practical jokes.*

US CRIPPLES

At the end of three weeks of classes the medical students knew
my tendency to use humor. So I told them, "Next Monday
morning, Jerry, you go to the fourth floor and keep the elevator
doors open. Tommy, you stand on the stairwell and look down to
the ground floor. When you see me walking up the steps, signal
Jerry to release the elevator doors, and Sam, you be on the ground
floor pressing the elevator button. In the meantime, spread the
rumor that on next Monday morning Dr. Erickson is going to pull
one of his gags on the class."

They did good work spreading the rumor. Next Monday all
the class was there, including a boy with a prosthesis. That student had been very sociable, outgoing, friendly with everybody,
during his freshman year. In his sophomore year everybody liked
him and he liked everybody; he was always socializing. He was a
good student, well respected, well liked by everybody. In his
sophomore year he lost a leg in an automobile accident through
no fault of his. When he was fitted with an artificial leg, he
became very withdrawn, oversensitive. The dean had warned me
about that boy being withdrawn and oversensitive, but still a good

student, how he had dropped all his old friendliness, never returned a greeting, never greeted anybody, just kept his nose in his books and minded his own business.

I told the dean to give me a few weeks to let the class get acquainted with me and then I'd take care of that chap. On that Monday, with Jerry holding the elevator doors open and Tommy stationed at the head of the stairwell, I found the class all on the ground floor waiting for me at seven-thirty. I engaged in social chitchat about the weather and what was going on in Detroit and then I said, "What's the matter with your thumb, Sam? Is it weak? Push that elevator button."

He said, "I have been."

I said, "Maybe your thumb is so weak, you ought to use two thumbs."

He said, "I tried that too, but that damn janitor is so worried about getting his pail and mops down, he's probably holding the elevator doors open."

I talked a while and then told Sam, "Push that elevator again."

Sam obliged. No sound of the elevator coming. Finally, at five minutes of eight I turned to the student with the artificial leg and said, "Let's us cripples hobble upstairs and leave the elevator for the able-bodied."

"Us cripples" started hobbling upstairs. Tommy signaled to Jerry; Sam pushed the button. The able-bodied waited for the elevator. Us cripples hobbled upstairs. At the end of the hour, that student was socializing again—with a new identity. He belonged to the professorial group: "Us cripples." I was a professor; I had a bad leg; he identified with me; I identified with him. So with that new status he regained all his outgoing ways. He was socializing at the end of the hour.

Often, simply by the changing of a frame of reference, something can be accomplished. The elaborate planning here, with the

*use of accomplices, is similar to the preparation a magician puts
into his performance. It is also similar to the preparation leading
up to a practical joke.*

BLANK PAPER

Significant therapy can often be done very, very simply, even
though the therapeutic task looks to be huge. One year a new
dean took his palce at the medical school. He called me into his
office and said, "I'm the new dean here and I brought with me
a protégé of mine. Now this protégé of mine is an absolute gem
because he's the most brilliant student I've ever encountered. He
is gifted in pathology. He understands pathology and is very
interested in slides, but he hates all psychiatrists. And he has a
very sharp tongue. He will insult you from all directions. He'll take
every chance he can to annoy you."

I said, "Don't worry, Dean. I'll handle him."

The Dean said, "Well, you will be the first ever to handle
him."

And so the first day I introduced myself and told the class I
was not like other medical-school professors. Other medical-
school professors thought that their course was the most important course given in medical school. But I was quite different.

I didn't think any such nonsense. It just happened that I *knew*
my course was the most important. That was taken in by the class
very nicely. And then I said, "For those only mildly interested in
psychiatry, I offer a list of about forty extracurricular references
for them to read. And for those that have some considerable
interest in psychiatry, I offer a list of about fifty references they
can read. And for those who are really interested, I offer a list of
about sixty outside-reading topics."

And then I told the whole class to write a review of a certain syllabus on psychiatry and hand in their reviews next Monday.

Next Monday, that student who hated psychiatry stood in line. Each student passed in his review. That student handed me a blank sheet of paper.

I said, "Without reading your review, I notice you made two mistakes: you haven't dated it, and you haven't signed it. So, turn it in next Monday. And remember, a book review is like reading pathology slides."

I got one of the most competent book reviews I've ever had in my life.

And the dean said, "How on earth did you make a Christian out of that heathen?"

I took him completely by surprise.

Erickson might have seen the blank paper as an attempt to insult him, and he always pointed out, "Never take an insult." However, by refusing to see the student's behavior as an insult, Erickson took him by surprise. By pointing out "two mistakes," he maintained his position of authority. And by directing the student to look for similarities between a book review and reading pathology slides, he applied some basic teaching principles— initiating motivation and connecting new learnings with older ones. By keeping up the pretense that the blank page was an actual book review, Erickson was also demonstrating the "join the patient" principle. We see this applied, very literally, in the next tale.

RUTH

At Worcester Hospital, the superintendent remarked one day, "I wish *somebody* could find some way of handling Ruth."

I inquired about Ruth, a very pretty, petite twelve-year-old girl, very winning in her ways. You couldn't help liking her. She was so nice in her behavior. And all the nurses warned every new nurse who came to work there, "Keep away from Ruth. She'll tear your dress; break your arm or your foot!"

The new nurses didn't believe that of sweet, winsome twelve-year-old Ruth. And Ruth would beg the new nurse, "Oh, would you please bring me an ice-cream cone and some candy from the store?"

The nurse would do it and Ruth would accept the candy and thank the nurse very sweetly, and with a single karate chop break the nurse's arm, or rip her dress off, or kick her in the shins, or jump on her foot. Standard, routine behavior for Ruth. Ruth enjoyed it. She also liked to tear the plaster off the walls periodically.

I told the superintendent I had an idea, and asked if I could handle the case. He listened to my ideas and said, "I think that will work, and I know just the nurse who'll be glad to help you."

One day I got a call. "Ruth is on a binge again." I went to the ward. Ruth had torn the plaster off the walls. *I* tore off the bed clothes. I helped her destroy the bed. I helped her break windows. I had spoken to the hospital engineer before going to the ward; it was cold weather. Then I suggested, "Ruth, let's pull that steam register away from the wall and twist off the pipe." And so I sat down on the floor and we tugged away. We broke the register off the pipe.

I looked around the room and said, "There's nothing more we can do here. Let's go to another room."

And Ruth said, "Are you sure you ought to do this, Dr. Erickson?"

I said, "Sure, it's fun, isn't it? I think it is."

As we walked down the corridor to another room there was a nurse standing in the corridor. As we came abreast of her, I stepped over and ripped her uniform and her slip off so she stood in her panties and bra.

And Ruth said, "Dr. Erickson, you shouldn't do a thing like that." She rushed into the room and got the torn bedsheets, and wrapped them around the nurse.

She was a good girl after that. I really showed her what her behavior was like. Of course the nurse was an experienced nurse, and she enjoyed the episode as much as I did. All the nurses were horrified. All the rest of the staff was horrified at my behavior. Only the superintendent and I agreed that my behavior was right.

Ruth got even with me by escaping from the hospital, getting pregnant, delivering the child, putting it up for adoption. Then she voluntarily came back to the hospital and was a very good patient. A couple of years later she asked to be discharged, went to work as a waitress, met a young man, married him, became pregnant. To my knowledge, that marriage was happy long enough for two children to be born. Ruth was a good mother and a good citizen.

Often a patient can be shocked out of wrong behavior. That's true for the neurotics and for the psychotics.

SALAAM

The first year I was on the faculty at Wayne State Medical School, two particular things happened. In my class there was a girl who had been late to every class in high school. She was called up by teachers, and always promised prettily that she would be on time next time. And she apologized so sincerely. She was late to every class in high school and she was a straight-A student. She was always so apologetic, so full of believable promises.

She was late for every class in college, bawled out by every instructor and every professor. She always apologized prettily and sincerely and always promised to do better in the future—and kept on being late. She was a straight-A student in college.

Then she went to medical school and she was late to every class, to every lecture, to every laboratory. So her fellow students cussed her out for being late, for holding them up in laboratory work. And she went her merry way, apologizing and promising.

Now, someone on the faculty of the medical school who knew me said when they found out I was appointed to the faculty, "Wait till she hits Erickson's class! There will be a terrific explosion! It will be heard the world around!"

On my first day I arrived at seven-thirty for my eight o'clock lecture and all the class was waiting, including Anne, the tardy one.

So at eight we all filed into the auditorium, except Anne. Each side of the auditorium had an aisle. There was an aisle at the back of the room, there was an aisle on the west side. The students were not listening to my lecture. They were looking at the door. I lectured, undisturbed, and when the door opened, very gently and softly and slowly, in walked Anne, twenty minutes late. All the students made a quick jerk with their heads and looked at me. They saw me gesture for them to stand and they all understood my language.

I salaamed to Anne as she walked from the door across the front of the room, down across the back of the room, halfway up the other side, and then took her seat, a seat on the middle aisle. And all the class silently salaamed her all the way. At the end of the class, there was a wild rush to get outside. Anne and I were the last to leave the auditorium. I was talking about Detroit weather, or some subject like that, and as we walked down the corridor, a janitor silently salaamed her; some undergraduate students came down the corridor and silently salaamed her; the dean stepped out of his office and salaamed her. His secretary came out and salaamed her; all day long poor Anne got salaamed silently.

She was the first student in the class next day—and thereafter. She had withstood deans' rebukes, rebukes from all the professors, but silent salaaming she could not take.

Whereas other teachers had tried to change Anne's behavior by disciplining her, Erickson's approach was to congratulate her on her power. Salaaming was a way of showing obeisance. He made it clear to her that she was using her power in a reverse way. When she could understand this, she could determine how she was going to use her power constructively.

Other people had tried to control her by verbal means and she proved that she could not be verbally controlled. Erickson used a nonverbal approach, which led her to realize that she was using her control in a self-hurting way. She could direct her controlling tendencies in more constructive ways. As in all cases, the power to change resided in her. Erickson set up a situation in which the change could happen.

Erickson's attitude indicated his belief that he could deal incisively with whatever situation arose. If the situation called for confrontation, he knew that he could do that. If it called for kindness, he could be kind. If it called for sharpness, he knew he could be sharp. The subliminal message Erickson is giving us is that he had confidence in his ability to handle situations. We are free to identify with this feeling ourselves and to be more assertive.

GLOBUS HYSTERICUS

I had a nurse come in. I had known her slightly. She was one of those know-it-all nurses. She'd been discharged from hospital after hospital because she told the doctors what to do. She told them the diagnosis and the treatment.

And she came in and said that she had globus hystericus, a lump in her throat, and it was very distressing. I had her describe the distress. And she described the pain. I reached my own conclusions and said, "You do not have globus hystericus. You have an ulcer of the stomach, at the duodenal end."

She said, "Don't be ridiculous."

I said, "I'm not, you are."

She said, "I'll prove to you I don't have a stomach ulcer." She went to three different radiologists, all of whom confirmed my diagnosis. And she came back very angry and said, "You're right. I saw the X rays myself and they all agreed. What are you going to advise me to do?"

I said, "You're Armenian. You like spicy food. You have a sister who calls you up every day and has a long telephone conversation with you. You have a niece who calls you up every day, has a long telephone conversation. *Hang up* on your sister and your niece. They *both* give you a pain in your stomach. And enjoy your food."

A month later she got new X rays from all three radiologists. No trace of an ulcer. And that was all the recommendation, "Enjoy your food, hang up on your sister and your niece."

Her favorite expression was "I can't swallow this, I can't swallow that." That's why she reached the diagnosis of globus hystericus. Her description of the pain indicated it must be a duodenal ulcer. But she knew I was wrong. Three independent radiologists convinced her I was *right.*

Oddly enough, this "know-it-all" nurse who was so bossy with doctors could not be assertive with her own sister and niece. Erickson sets an example of assertiveness with his own attitude. In fact, in this story he appears to be approaching arrogance as he assumes the "know-it-all" posture. However, he apparently felt that he had to do this in order to persuade this woman to take

direction. With another patient, Linda, whose treatment I wit-
nessed, Erickson had given her instructions to climb Squaw Peak.
At first she resisted this direction, but then, one day, in the middle
of a session in which Erickson was meeting with about ten stu-
dents, she knocked on the door. She reported that she had
climbed Squaw Peak, as he had ordered. Also, as ordered, she
came to report this to him. He simply dismissed her, without
further comment.

After she had left, the group was interested in why Erickson
had asked her to climb Squaw Peak. Did he want her to "get in
touch with her own feelings"? Did he want her to accomplish a
task successfully? His answer, surprisingly, was "So she would
obey me." Erickson often pointed out that it was important that
the therapist direct the treatment. If he could not obtain obedi-
ence in at least one specific area, he would feel that there was no
point in continuing treatment. In the case of the nurse, it was
important for him to know that she would follow his suggestion
and actually hang up on her sister and her niece.

OATS

I spent one summer grubbing up brush on ten acres of land.
My father plowed it that fall and replanted it, replowed it in the
spring, and planted it into oats. And the oats grew very well and
we hoped to get an excellent crop. Late that summer, on a Thursday evening, we went over to see how that crop was getting along,
when we could harvest it. My father examined the individual oat
stalks and said, "Boys, this is not going to be a bumper crop of
thirty-three bushels per acre. It will be at least a hundred bushels
per acre. And they will be ready to harvest next Monday."

And we were walking along happily thinking about a thousand
bushels of oats and what it meant to us financially. It started to

sprinkle. It rained all night Thursday, all day Friday, all night Friday, all day Saturday, all night Saturday, all day Sunday, and in the early morning on Monday the rain ceased. When we were finally able to wade through the water to that back field, the field was totally flat; there weren't any upright oats.

My father said, "I hope enough of the oats are ripe enough so that they will sprout. In that way we will have some green feed for the cattle this fall—and next year is another year."

And that's really being oriented to the future, and very, very necessary in farming.

This theme—that tomorrow is another day, that the sun will rise again tomorrow, that no matter what happens it is not the end of the world, that no matter how flattened out you feel there's always the basis for some new growth and fresh beginnings—is a common one in the teaching tales. It's a great source of inspiration and it is certainly an effective antidote to self-pity.

GROWTH

My son Lance came into the office and said, "Will I always be a string-bean Maypole?" He was very slender, very tall, very thin.

I said, "Your destiny as a teenager is to be a string-bean Maypole. And you can look forward to the day when you walk into the office, hand me your jacket, and say, 'Get lost, Dad.' "

And one day he walked into the office, a grin on his face, handed me his jacket, and said, "Get lost, Dad." I put on his jacket; the sleeves were too long. They covered my hands and the shoulders were too wide.

Erickson is using an attribute that appears negative and is pointing out its positive aspect. In every negative, he can find a positive. Any good therapist does this. Erickson just does it better than most. So Erickson reframes being a string bean into being taller than Dad and knows that this will evoke a good feeling. Lance can look forward to being taller than Dad, to a time when Dad will get lost in Lance's jacket.

Jeffrey Zeig pointed out to me that Erickson always had a goal. Zeig said, "I went over to him one day, and out of the blue I said to him, 'What's your goal?' Without hesitation Erickson said, 'To see Roxanna's [his daughter] baby.' He knew exactly what I was saying. He did not bat an eyelash. I knew that he would name something in the future." Zeig went on, "He had this positive orientation to the future. It was not an obsession, it was like a light that draws a moth to it. He did not become obsessed with it, but it was out there and it pulled him along."

13. Teaching Values and Self-Discipline

I DON'T HAS TO

One Sunday, we were reading the newspaper, all of us. Kristi walked up to her mother, grabbed the newspaper, and threw it on the floor. Her mother said, "Kristi, that wasn't very nice. Pick up the paper and give it back to Mother. Tell her you're sorry."

"I don't has to," Kristi said.

Every member of the family gave Kristi the same advice and got the same reply. So I told Betty to pick her up and put her in the bedroom. I lay down on the bed and Betty dropped Kristi on the bed beside me. Kristi looked at me contemptuously. She started to scramble off, but I had a hold on her ankle. She said, "Wet woose!"

I said, "I don't has to."

And that lasted four hours. She kicked and struggled. Pretty soon she freed one ankle; I got hold of the other. It was a desperate fight—like a silent fight between two titans. At the end of four hours, she knew that she was the loser and she said, "I pick up the paper and give it to Mommy."

And that's where the axe fell. I said, "You don't *has* to."

So she threw her brain into higher gear and said, "I pick up the paper. I give it to Mommy. I tell Mommy sorry."

And I said, "You don't *has* to."

And she shifted into full gear. "I pick up paper. I *want* pick up paper. I *want* tell Mommy sorry."

I said, "Fine."

Ten years later, my two younger girls yelled at their mother. I called the girls and said, "Stand on the rug. I don't think it's very nice to yell at Mother. Stand there and think it over and see if you agree with me."

Kirsti said, "I could stand here all night."

Roxie said, "I don't think it's very nice to yell at Ma and I will go and apologize to her."

I continued writing on a manuscript. An hour later, I turned to Kristi. Even one hour is fatiguing. I turned back, and wrote another hour. Turned back and said, "Even the hands of the clock seem to be moving very slowly." Half an hour later I turned and said, "I think that was a very stupid remark you made to Mother. I think it's very stupid to yell at your ma."

She collapsed in my lap and said, "So do I," and sobbed.

Ten years without disciplining a child—two to twelve. At fifteen I disciplined her once more, that's all. Three times only.

In his article "The Identification of a Secure Reality," published in Family Process, *Erickson pointed out that "Reality, security, and the definitions of boundaries and limitations constitute important considerations in the growth of understanding in childhood. . . . When one is small, weak and intelligent, living in an undefined world of intellectual and emotional fluctuations, one seeks to learn what is really strong, secure and safe."*

Erickson could have quit after Kristi had "given in," but he persisted until she could say, "I wants to." She had then changed the "has to" into a "wants to." She had internalized the socially desirable activity. In this story Erickson described, as succinctly as has ever been done, the development of conscience or superego.

He also emphasized the importance of early "definition of boundaries and limitations." With this early "strong, secure" disciplining, it was necessary to discipline Kristi only two more times in fifteen years. The early lesson was well learned.

GARBAGE

Children have poor memories, but I have an excellent memory for them.

Robert announced one day, "I'm old enough and big enough and strong enough to carry out the garbage every night."

I expressed my doubts. He staunchly defended his ability. I said, "All right, next Monday you can begin."

He carried it out Monday and Tuesday, but forgot Wednesday. On Thursday I reminded him and he took the garbage out, but forgot it on Friday and Saturday. So, that Saturday I gave him a lot of active games, which he enjoyed immensely and which were tiring. And then as a special favor, I let him stay awake as late as he wished. At one o'clock he said, "I think I want to go to bed now."

I let him go to bed. By some coincidence, I awakened at three o'clock. I wakened Robert and I offered apologies all over the map for not reminding him to take out the garbage that night. Would he please dress and take out the garbage? So, with great reluctance, he dressed. I apologized again for not reminding him, and he took out the garbage.

He took his clothes off, put on his pajamas, and got back into bed. I was sure he was sound asleep. I wakened him again. This time I was even more apologetic. I told him I didn't know how that piece of garbage got overlooked in the kitchen. Would he please dress and take that garbage out. He took it out, to the garbage can in the alley. He walked back, thinking hard, and reached the back porch. Then he turned and dashed back to the alley and checked the cover of the garbage can to make sure that he had put it on correctly.

He stopped when he came in and gave the kitchen the once-over again, before he went back to his bedroom. I was still apologizing. He went back to bed and he never again forgot to take out the garbage.

In fact, Robert remembered this lesson so well that when I mentioned that I was writing the story, he groaned reminiscently.

HEIDI-HO, THE SIX-YEAR-OLD KLEPTOMANIAC

A couple came to see me, in despair, asking, "What can we do with our six-year-old daughter? She steals from us. She steals from our friends and from her friends. When she goes shopping with her mother, she steals from the store. We sent her to a girls' camp for the day and she came home with things belonging to other girls, things that even had other girls' names on them. She tells lies about her mother buying things for her. She insists that they are hers. Can anything be done with a kleptomaniac at that age? With a shoplifter at that age? With a liar who is only six years old?"

I told them I'd take care of it. I wrote a letter to the girl:

"Dear Heidi-Ho, I am your six-year-old-growing-up fairy. Every child has a growing-up fairy. Nobody sees a growing-up fairy. You've never seen me. Maybe you'd like to know what I look like. I've got eyes on top of my head, in front of my head, and under my chin. That's so I can see everything that my child, for whom I am a growing-up fairy, does.

"Now, I have been watching you slowly learning things. I've

been very pleased with the way you learned a lot of things. Some things are harder to learn than others. And I have ears too. I don't have any ears on top of my head, because they would interfere with my eyes seeing everything. I have ears in swivel joints on my cheeks so I can turn them in any direction I wish, to hear everything, in all directions. And I have a lot of ears here down my neck and side and all over my hind legs, all down my tail. And the ear on the end of my tail is very large—it is on a swivel joint. (Ask your dad to tell you what a swivel joint is.) So I can turn that ear in any direction I wish, so I can hear everything that you say or any noise that you make, when you are doing things.

"I've got one right foot and three left front feet. I use two left front feet to walk with—the outside ones. The inside foot has thirty-two toes on it. That's why my writing is poor, because I can't remember which toes to put the pencil between. And of course I walk twice as fast on my left side as I do on my right side. So I can keep going in a straight line. I have seven hind feet— three of my left hind feet and three of my right hind feet, so I can keep my right side going just as fast as my left side goes. And I like to go around barefoot, and you know how hot it gets in summer in Phoenix. So I wear shoes on two of my seven hind feet. I keep the others bare."

I got an invitation for a seven-year-old birthday and I had to decline attending because I was a *six*-year-old-growing-up fairy. I didn't specialize in seven-year-olds, but was a *six*-year-old-growing-up fairy, who would keep watching her and listening to her. And that story kept her straight.

In supplying input from which a child can develop a healthy conscience, Erickson notably avoids prohibitions, "shoulds," and rules. He emphasizes, as always, the value of learning. As in the preceding story, the disciplinarian is not angry but, in fact, presents his teachings in an amusing way. In all his discipline stories,

Erickson is firm but not punitive, even though some readers may see his approach as punitive or as a battle of wills. Actually, his purpose is to help the child develop his own sense of will and autonomy.

In this case of a young child who had already been labeled a kleptomaniac, Erickson does not become involved with the "dynamics" of kleptomania. He decides, instead, that the child needs an internalized superego and, through the medium of a letter written to appeal to a child, he supplies that internal guardian and watchdog.

EASTER BUNNY LETTERS

One mother brought her seven-year-old and said, "Her two older siblings have shaken her belief in Santa Claus—and she is desperately hanging on to her belief in the Easter Bunny. And I'd like to have her believe in the Easter Bunny one more year, because by the time she is eight she won't believe it, but she wants to believe in it now."

I wrote this girl an Easter Bunny letter, telling her about all my hard times, hopping around and getting my feet sore, trying to find the hardest-boiled Easter egg in the world. I thought she deserved that. I wrote, "And I miscalculated when I jumped over a cactus and got some stickers where it *hurt.* I was nearly bitten by a rattlesnake. I got a ride with a wild burro. It was a kindly burro, but an awfully stupid burro. He took me in the wrong direction and I had to hop all the way back. Then I wasn't smart enough to know better than to take a ride with a jack rabbit on a dead run, taking me in the wrong direction and I had to hop all the way back again!"

I said, "I'm not going to take any more rides. I think hitchhiking is very bad."

And she took that Easter Bunny letter to "show-and-tell" at school and at Easter got the hardest-boiled egg in the world—an onyx egg!

And people are still calling me up, asking me to play Santa Claus over the phone with their children, the same way I did when their parents were my patients.

Three little girls for six weeks every morning hopped out of bed and rushed to the letter slot in the door to get their letter from the Easter Bunny. I sent them daily accounts of my travels. And always the stationery was different. And they got the hardest-boiled eggs in the world. And I got a lot of my Easter Bunny letters taken to "show-and-tell."

Erickson demonstrates the principle that the therapist can supply what is needed or missing. In "Heidi-Ho," the young child needed an internalized superego. In "The Easter Bunny Letters," the child needed evidence that Easter Bunnies existed. If bunnies can write letters, they must exist! Strictly speaking, this tale is not aimed at instilling values, yet this kind of story, heard when young, may predispose a person to value fantasy and whimsy later in life.

ROBERT—HE DOES IT WELL

When my son Robert was seven years old, he and a truck tried to use the street at the same time and he lost. The police picked me up to identify the boy with a spelling paper in his pocket with the name "Bobby" on it. I looked at Robert in the Good Samaritan Hospital and told them, "Yes, that is my son." I asked the emergency-room doctor, "What's the damage?" He said, "Both thighs are broken. The pelvis is fractured. The skull is fractured and he has a concussion.

We're checking him for internal injuries at the present time."

I waited until they told me he had no internal injuries. Then I asked, "What's the prognosis?

And the doctor said, "Well, *if* he lives forty-eight hours, he *may* have a chance to live."

I went home, called all the family together and said, "We all know Robert. We know that *when Robert has to do something he does it.* He does it very well. Now, at the present time, Robert is in Good Samaritan Hospital. A truck ran over him and broke both his legs, fractured his pelvis, fractured his skull, and bumped his brains so bad that he has what is called a concussion. So he doesn't know anybody. And he can't think straight. And we'll have to wait forty-eight hours before we'll know if Robert will live. Now, we all know Robert. When he does things, he does them well. You can always take pride in what Robert does.

"If you want to shed a couple of tears, it's all right. But I think it would be very disrespectful of Robert if you did a *lot* of crying. Out of respect for Robert, I think you ought to do all your home chores. I think you ought to eat a good supper. I think you ought to do all your homework. And I want you to go to bed on time. Go to sleep on time and sleep restfully all night. You owe Robert that respect."

A couple of the kids shed a couple of tears, ate a good meal and did all their chores, then washed dishes, did their homework. They went to bed on time.

In forty-eight hours we knew that Robert was going to live.

I told them all that we ought to leave Robert alone in the hospital where he had a very hard job—that is, getting well. Now, if we went over and visited him, it would take a lot of his energy and he needed that energy to get well. I didn't know it, but my wife would slip over to the hospital every day, walk in, sit down quietly by the bed. Sometimes Robert would turn over, turn his back to her. Sometimes he'd tell her, "Go home." Sometimes he'd ask her a question or two, and then tell her to go home. She did whatever he told her to.

We sent Robert plenty of presents. We always had the nurse deliver them. We never gave him anything personally.

I'd go over, go to the nurses' station, look through the window so I could see how Robert was getting along. Robert didn't know I was there.

The accident happened on December 5, and Robert came home from the hospital in a body cast, late in March. The stretcher men who brought him into the house almost dropped him. And Robert was very excited. As he was brought in to the living room Robert said, "I'm so glad I've got parents like you. Never once did you come to the hospital. And all the other poor kids, their parents came every afternoon and made them cry. Then they came every evening, and made the poor kids cry again. And on Sundays it was awful. I just hated those parents who wouldn't let their kids get well."

During my internship, I took the temperature, breathing rate, pulse, an hour before patients received their visitors. An hour after the visitors left I took their pulse, respiration, and blood pressure. Every time a patient had a visitor, his temperature went up. His breathing rate became exaggerated and the blood pressure increased. I made up my mind then, if I ever had children or a wife in the hospital, I wouldn't visit until I knew it would be safe for the blood pressure, heart rate, and their breathing, and for their temperature. Patients in a hospital need to use their strength to get well and not to make their relatives who are well and healthy feel better.

This story was told in response to the question, "Do you believe that it's necessary to feel the pain of grief or loss? Shouldn't that be worked through?" Most readers will feel that Erickson's behavior was strange and cold for a parent. Yet he sincerely believed that when a person is seriously ill he should be left alone to do his own "work" of healing, and that visitors are enervating. He is obviously overstating his case somewhat, since he mentions that Mrs. Erickson did sit by the child's bed every day ("I didn't know it"). And he, himself, apparently could not avoid going to the nurses' station frequently ("so I could see how Robert was getting along"). Also, the Erickson children must have learned very early that they were expected not to make a fuss about illness and loss. They took pride in being self-sufficient.

After hearing this story, a student asked Erickson rather angrily why he didn't visit his son and use some of his hypnosis on him, "to help him get better faster." Erickson answered, "The kids couldn't have lived with me all their lives without learning something. I taught the kids the unimportance of pain and importance of physical comfort. For example, when Roxanna scratched her knee, she was really announcing it to the whole city. Her mother came out and looked at it; so did I. Her mother said, 'Mother will kiss it here and here and then right on top, so all the pain will go away.' It's marvelous how anesthetic a mother's kiss can be."

He is saying indirectly that for small scratches, it is all right to use "motherly" comforting. In serious, life-threatening situations, it is best to leave the patient alone as much as possible. In his response, Erickson is also correcting a serious misconception about self-hypnosis. He is saying that it is not necessary to go through ritualistic induction in order to achieve self-hypnotic effects. Simple awareness of "the unimportance of pain and the importance of physical comfort" can produce the same effect as hypnotic induction in which the patient is told these things by a "hypnotist." In other words, if one has accepted a value or belief, the effect on his responses is as permanent as if he had been "hypnotized" into acceptance.

Erickson is not only conveying his ideas about visiting the sick.

*He is actually saying that the parent or the helper must stand by
and be available when called for; help is offered only to the extent
that the recipient wants it. When Robert told Betty Erickson to
"go home," she would do so.*

*If we examine the story on an intrapsychic level, we see that
the "child" again determines what is best for himself. Interfer-
ence by the adults simply delays healing or growth. This delay is
manifested in very basic ways. Erickson's tales often focus on
blood pressure, heart rate, and breathing. This strategy is part of
his indirect hypnotic inductions. In this tale, he is pointing out
that there is a disruption of natural physiological responses—of
natural functioning—when parents impose their anxieties on a
child. Or when the "parent" in an individual—the "inner
sounds"—are operating on an anxious level. When this happens,
"the kids cry." Intrapsychically, we have a feeling of sadness or
self-hate, in Horney's terms, when the "shoulds" are too stringent. In the commentary at the end of the story, however, Erickson emphasizes the fact that the "mother" can accomplish marvelous results with a kiss. In other words, the ability to be a good
mother to ourselves, loving ourselves, can have an "anesthetic"
effect, that is, it can relieve inner pain and doubt. This is similar
to the ideas expressed by Antonia Wenkart in her papers on
"Acceptance," and by Theodore Rubin in* Compassion and Self-
Hate.

*And, of course, therapists must not interfere when their pa-
tients are doing good work.*

SATURDAY CLASSES ON SUNDAY

A medical student forgot to attend Saturday classes. He always
awakened Saturday morning, went out, and played golf, always
completely forgetting it was still a class day. Until he hit my class.

I explained to him that the week has seven days, that Saturday was a school day, and I would give him a lesson, not on Saturday, but on Sunday, which was not a regular class day, and he would remember that Saturday was a class day thereafter.

So I said, "Tomorrow morning, on Sunday, at 8 A.M., come twenty miles out to Wayne County Hospital, walk into my office, and wait for me. If I'm a few minutes late, don't think I've forgotten you; I haven't. So just stick around for the assignment, and when you've completed the assignment, you can go home at four o'clock."

You know, I forgot I told him that. And he sat in my office all day, until four o'clock.

He came to my office the next Sunday at 8 A.M., praying I would remember. Again I had forgotten.

The third Sunday, I gave him a nice, interesting series of patients to interview. They were so interesting that he didn't want to go home at four o'clock. He stayed until five o'clock. He never again forgot a Saturday class.

The same principle is applied here as in the story "I Don't Has To"—the tables are turned. Since the student forgot to attend the Saturday classes, Erickson "forgets" to attend the scheduled meetings on Sundays. Why did the student dutifully travel twenty miles, to arrive at 8 A.M. on Sundays, even after Erickson failed to show? We can only speculate about this. Perhaps he was pleased to be singled out for individual attention. Perhaps the "ordeal" aspect of Erickson's "prescription" appealed to him. Other patients and students certainly tended to carry out Erickson's ordeals. In any case, Erickson finally rewarded the student by giving him some interesting patients to interview, so that the experience became a positive one. Subsequently, the student was able, and perhaps eager, to turn up at Saturday classes, anticipating further positive contacts with Erickson.

Note that this discipline was not applied in a punitive or vindictive way. On some level, the student knew, just as Kristi did, that Erickson was not angry, but was really helping him to develop self-discipline.

JILL, HER OWN STYLE

I received a letter from my one-and-a-half-year-old grand-daughter; her mother did the writing. One-and-a-half-year-old Jill went to the swimming pool for the first time. And she cried when her foot got wet. She cried and clung to her mother when her hand got wet. And finally she cried and cried and cried, and clung tightly until her mother let *Jill* direct the operation entirely.

Now she's planning her next trip to the pool, and teaching mother, "Let me deal with it on my terms."

All my grandchildren have had a different approach to life, and they are very decisive. When they want to do something, they do it but *they do it in their own style.* And their mother is able to describe it in detail. I'm keeping their letters so they can eventually be bound into a volume for the kids when they are sixteen or seventeen and are bemoaning the lack of intelligence in their parents.

The important phrase is "they do it in their own style." Erickson applies this principle to children as well as patients. It is always up to the patients to choose their own solution. This reinforces a child's or a patient's tendency toward respecting his own values and learning self-discipline.

SPANKING

One day my son Lance came home from grade school and he said, "Daddy, all the other kids at school get spankings and I haven't ever had a spanking. So I want a spanking."

I said, "There's no reason to spank you."

He said, "I'll give you one," and he went outside and broke one of the windows of the hospital.

He came back and asked me, "Now, can I get a spanking?"

I said, "No, the proper thing to do is replace the pane of glass for the window. A spanking won't do that."

He was disgusted and went out and broke another window-pane. He said, "Now will you spank me?"

I said, "No, I will replace the windowpane." In all, he broke seven panes of glass. While he was out breaking the seventh pane, I was on the balcony of our apartment. I lined up seven of his cast-iron trucks on the railing. He came in to announce, "I broke the seventh pane of glass; now will you spank me?"

I said, "No, replace the panes is what I'll do." Then I said, "Now, here are seven of your trucks on the railing. I'm going to start the first one rolling down the railing. I hope it will stop and not roll off, crash, and break on the sidewalk below. Oh, that's too bad! Maybe the second one will stop."

He lost seven trucks. About three weeks later he came home from school very happy. I seized him, put him over my knees, and spanked him. He said, "Why are you doing that?"

I said, "I seem to remember that you asked me to spank you. I didn't meet your wishes."

He said, "I know better now."

Of course I didn't spank him very hard. It was a token spanking.

Erickson is illustrating a principle he applied both to disciplining children and to treating patients. He does not give what is asked for. Rather, he gives what is called for. And he gives it when he deems it to be appropriate. We saw this in his teaching Robert to fulfill his promise to be responsible for taking out the garbage.

In that case, he "reminded" Robert in the middle of the night, knowing that this type of reminder would be remembered. And we see something similar in the next story, where he has someone do something at a time that is inconvenient for him.

SLAMMING DOORS

My grandson Douglas came into my office while I was conducting a teaching seminar. After showing off his new sneakers he left. About forty minutes later he returned, while I was in the middle of a demonstration of deepening of trance.

I told him, "Run along, Douglas," and he answered impudently, "I couldn't hear you."

"Run along," I repeated, "go into the house."

Douglas left, slamming the door. Obviously he didn't like that. He shouldn't have slammed the door. Now, if he were my child, I would graciously ask him, for no apparent reason, "Please slam the door." I would do this while he was busy looking at a picture book. He'd wonder why, but would obediently do it. I'd thank him and ask him to slam the door again. He'd slam it again, wondering. And I'd ask him to slam the door again.

He'd say, "But I want to read my book."

"Well, just slam it again," I'd insist.

He'd slam it again and pretty soon he'd inquire why I had asked him to slam the door. I'd remind him of the original slamming and say, "The way you slammed the door made me think you *liked* to slam doors."

His answer would be, "I really don't like to slam doors."

You learn very rapidly in situations that are not to your inclination.

As in "Spanking," Erickson supplies the right medicine. In this situation, having Douglas slam the door when it was not to his "inclination" would lead him to discover that he really didn't "like" to slam doors. It would drive home to him that the door slamming had been unconsciously determined or reactive, rather than something he "wanted" to do. In the future, presumably, he would exercise more control over his actions, doing what he really "wanted" to do. At least he would have more awareness of what he was doing.

We have seen Erickson apply this principle in many different situations—with children, with neurotic patients, and even with psychotics. He would either "mirror" the patient's undesirable behavior or would have the patient repeat it, under his orders, as with "symptom prescription." He never resorted to sarcasm, irritability, or hostility. His attitude could best be described as a "wondering" one: "I wonder what will happen if I ask Douglas to slam the door?"

Erickson himself maintained that "childlike" wondering attitude, the attitude of the true scientist, to the very end.

Bibliography

Bandler, Richard, and Grinder, John. *Patterns of the Hypnotic Techniques of Milton H. Erickson, M.D.* Vol. 1. Cupertino, Calif.: Meta Publications, 1975.

Bateson, Gregory, and Mead, Margaret. "For God's Sake, Margaret." *Coevolution Quarterly* 10 (1976): 32.

Blake, William, *Complete Writings*. Edited by Geoffrey Keynes. London: Oxford University Press, 1957.

Bronowski, Jacob. *The Origins of Knowledge and Imagination.* New Haven: Yale University Press, 1978.

Daitzman, Reid J. *Mental Jogging.* New York: Marek, 1980.

DeRopp, Robert S. *The Master Game: Pathways to Higher Consciousness beyond the Drug Experience.* New York: Dell, 1968.

Erickson, Milton H., and Cooper, Linn. *Time Distortion in Hypnosis: An Experimental and Clinical Investigation,* 2d ed. Baltimore: Williams and Wilkins, 1959.

Erickson, Milton H. "The Identification of a Secure Reality." *Family Process* 1 (1962): 294–303.

Erickson, Milton H., Rossi, Ernest L., and Rossi, Shiela. *Hypnotic Realities. The Induction of Clinical Hypnosis and Forms of Indirect Suggestion.* New York: Irvington, 1976.

Erickson, Milton H., and Rossi, Ernest L. *Hypnotherapy: An Exploratory Casebook.* New York: Irvington, 1979.

Frankl, Viktor E. *From Death-Camp to Existentialism: A Psychiatrist's Path to a New Therapy,* trans. I. Lasch. Boston: Beacon Press, 1959.

Gordon, David. *Therapeutic Metaphors.* Cupertino, Calif.: Meta Publications, 1978.

Grinder, John, Delozier, Judith, and Bandler, Richard. *Patterns of the Hypnotic Techniques of Milton H. Erickson, M.D.* Vol. 2. Cupertino, Calif.: Meta Publications, 1977.

Haley, Jay, ed. *Advanced Techniques of Hypnosis and Therapy: Selected Papers of Milton Erickson, M.D.* New York: Grune and Stratton, 1967.

Haley, Jay. *Uncommon Therapy: The Psychiatric Techniques of Milton H. Erickson, M.D.* New York: Norton, 1973.

Lindner, Robert. *The Fifty-Minute Hour: A Collection of True Psychoanalytic Tales.* New York: Rinehart, 1955.

Mead, Margaret. "The Originality of Milton Erickson." *American Journal of Clinical Hypnosis* 20 (1977): 4–5.

Newell, Peter. *Topsys & Turvys.* New York: Dover, 1964.

Pearson, Robert E. "Communication and Motivation." *American Journal of Hypnosis* 9 (July 1966): 20ff.

Rabkin, Richard. *Strategic Psychotherapy: Brief and Symptomatic Treatment.* New York: Basic Books, 1977.

Rajneesh, Bhagwan Shree. *The Book of the Secrets 2.* New York: Harper Colophon Books, 1979.

Rosen, Sidney. "The Philosophy and Values of Milton H. Erickson," in Zeig, Jeffrey, ed., *Proceedings of the International Congress on Ericksonian Hypnosis and Psychotherapy.* New York: Brunner/Mazel, in press.

Rubin, Theodore. *Compassion and Self-Hate: An Alternative to Despair.* New York: McKay, 1975.

Schiff, Jacqui Lee. *Transactional Analysis Treatment of Psychosis. Cathexis Reader.* New York: Harper & Row, 1975.

Spiegel, Herbert, and Spiegel, David. *Trance and Treatment.* New York: Basic Books, 1978.

Watzlawick, Paul, Weakland, John, and Fisch, Richard. *Change: Principles of Problem Formation and Problem Resolution.* New York: Norton, 1974.

Watzlawick, Paul. *The Language of Change: Elements of Therapeutic Communication.* New York: Basic Books, 1978. p. 11.

Wenkart, Antonia. "Self Acceptance." *American Journal of Psychoanalysis* 15 (1955): 135–143.

Zeig, Jeffrey. *A Teaching Seminar with Milton H. Erickson, M.D.* New York: Brunner/Mazel, 1980.